MUSLIM F
THEIR RIGHTS
AND
DUTIES

Editor
A. HUSAIN

Adam Publishers & Distributors
New Delhi -2 (India)

Adam Publishers & Distributors
(Exporters & Importers)
1542, Pataudi House, Darya Ganj,
New Delhi-110002
Ph. : 23282550, 23284740,
Fax.: 23267510
E-mail : apd@bol.net.in,
  syedsajid_ali@rediffmail.com
website: www.adambooks.in

Edition-2009
ISBN : 81-7435-096-9
Price :

Printed & Bound in India
Published by :
S. Sajid Ali, for,
Adam Publishers & Distributors
1542, Pataudi House, Darya Ganj,
New Delhi-110002, India

Muslim Parents Their Rights and Duties

CONTENTS

Foreword

Parental Rights — 11
   Importance of Parents — 13
   Worldly Reward of Serving the Parents — 14
   Nice Behaviour with Parents — 15
   Respect and Reverence for Parents — 17
   Compensation for Parents — 18
   Compensation of Mother — 18
   Conduct of Hazrat Abu Hurairah with his Mother — 19
   Climax of the Obedience to Parents — 19
   When to Disobey the Parents — 21
   Advice of Hazrat Abu Darda — 23

Acts Beneficial for the Parents after their Death — 25
   1. Prayer for Deliverance — 25
   2. Fulfilment of Commitments and Wills of Parents — 26
   3. Pleasant Behaviour with Persons Close to the Parents — 27
   Behaviour of the Pious Compaions of the Holy Prophet — 27
   Fruits of Praying for the Deliverance of Parents — 29
   Looking at the Parents with Love and Affection — 29
   Financial Help to the Parents — 30
   Right of Father in the Wealth of his Son — 30
   The debts of Parents — 31
   Virtues of Serving the Parents — 31

Difference Between the Right of Parents	33
A Thought Provoking Dialogue	34
Consideration of the Maternal Affection	36
Carrying out the Wishes of the Mother	36
Nice Behaviour with Mother	37
Behaviour with the Foster Mother	37
Behaviour with the Non-Muslim Parents	39
The Infidel Mother of Hazrat S'ad	40
The Hadis about the Infidel Mother	41
Benefits the Nice Behaviour with Infidel Mother	41
Disobedience to Parent	43
The Worst Sin	43
The Letter of the Holy Prophet to the Yemenites	43
Advice of the Holy Prophet	44
Abusing the Parents	44
Rebuking the Parents	45
Ready Punishment for Disobeying the Parents	46
Nullifying the Virtues	46
Disobedience to Mother	47
Reward for Nice Treatment with the Parents-At a Glance	49
Rights of Children	51
Longing for Children	51
Expectations of Parents	52
Grievances of Parents in General	53
What the Parents should do	54
Consciousness about the Rights of Children	57

Importance of Children — 59
- Distinct Castle in Paradise — 60
- Children-A Continuous Source of Reward (Sadaqah-i-Jariah) — 61
- Killing Ones Own Children — 62
- Reasons for Killing Children — 63
- The Ordeal of the Innocent Girl — 66
- The Woeful True Story — 69
- Eradication of the Evil of Burying the Daughters Alive — 71
- Birth of a Girl — 72
- The Blessed Daughter — 75

Sustenance of Children — 79
- Natural Love for Children — 79
- A Muslim Mother — 80
- The Responsibilities in Nourishing the Children — 82
- Division of These Responsibilities — 83
- The Real Sphere of Women's Activities — 83
- The Best Role of Women — 87
- Widowed Mothers — 89
- Maternal Role of the Companions of the Holy Prophet — 90
- The Ideal Mother — 90
- Exemplary Sacrifice of Ummi-i-Hani — 92

Suckling the Children and Islam — 93
- Religious and Ethical Importance of Mother's Milk — 96
- Reward for Suckling Mothers — 98

Medical and Psychological Importance of Mother's Milk	99
Medical Opinion on Mother's Milk	99
Modern Research	100
Avoidance of Suckling the Children and Heart Diseases	101
Psychological Importance of Suckling the Children	102

Maintenance of Children 103

Meaning of Maintenance of Children	103
Attitude of Father in the Maintenance of Children	103
Islamic Concept of the Maintenance of Children	104
An Example of the Holy Prophet	105
Aqeeqah	105
Circumcision	107
Recompense for Suckling the Children	108
Maintenance of Children according to the Holy Quran	110
Maintenance of Children according to Hadith	111
Foremost Duty	111
Negligence of Maintaining the Children	112
The Most Rewarding Expenditure	113
The Most Fortunate father	114
The Mother who Spends upon Her Children	114

Sustenance of Daughters 117

The Enviable Reward	117
The Mother Who Deserves Heaven	118
A Daughter-Heaven of Parents	118
Warding a Destitute Daughter	119

The Revolutionary Change	119
An Interesting Scene	121
Pleasant Behaviour	122
Results of Maltreatment with the Children	123
A Revealing Incident	124
The Holy Quran and the Parental Behaviour	126
The Holy Prophet on Nice Treatment with Children	127
Unequal Treatment with Sons and Daughters	130
A Daughter-Shield from the Fire of Hell	133
Reward for Kindness	133

Behaviour of the Holy Prophet with his Children — 135
　Behaviour of the Holy Prophet with his Daughter — 135

Giving Good names to the Children — 139
　Good Names for Children — 140
　The Names Liked by Almighty Allah — 141
　Impression of Improper names — 142
　Respect for Names — 143
　Some Names Suggested by the Holy Prophet Muhammad (S.A.W.) — 143
　Bad Effects of Bad Names — 146
　Calling One by a Good Name — 147
　Calling by the Short Name — 147

Loving One's Children — 149
　Children - A Test for Parents — 150
　Cold Attitude Towards the Children — 152
　Loving the Children — 153

The Holy Prophet's Love for the Children	155
An Incident about Hazrat Yaqoob	156

Education & Training of Children — 157
- The Role of Mother — 157
- A Mother Transforms the Lives of People — 159

Making the Future of Children — 161
- Islam and Character Building of Children — 164
- Consideration for the Self-Respect of the Children — 166
- Time for Education of Children — 168
- Religious Education of Children — 170
- Telling True and Character Building Stories to the Children — 171
- The Salat (Prescribed Prayers) — 172

The Marriage of Children — 174
- Consequences of Unnecessary delay in Marriage — 174
- Finding a Suitable Match — 175
- Basic Standards for Selecting the Spouses — 176
- Advice of the Holy Prophet — 177

FOREWORD

Social Structure throughout the world is crumbling down to pieces and virtually a social anarchy is prevailing every where. Family life in the West has been completely ruined and the sanctity of relations is fastly disappearing. It is a pity that Muslim society which once introduced culture and civilization to the East and the West and dominated the world for centuries, is now tempted to adopt the western civilization which is now immolating itself. Now it is the need of the hour that all those persons who feel to save the society from its total destruction should rise to the occasion and strive for its salvation.

The basic unit of the society is family. The first step to save the society is to establish the family on the right footing. Islam has provided an elaborate scheme for the establishment of a sound family life. Holy Quran and the Sunnah are replete with the comprehensive teachings for the betterment and preservation of the family.

With this end in view, we are presenting, this book. 'Muslim Parents — Their Rights and Duties — for our readers. It contains not only the comprehensive principles and teachings of Islam on the subject, it also invites all the family members to follow them ZEALOUSLY, sincerely and persistently. Practical examples from the Life of the Holy Prophet (S.A.W.) and his pious companions have been extensively quoted so that it may prove a practical guide for the readers.

We are also grateful to our friend, Mr. Manzoor Ahmad Khan, who rendered the manuscript into English and helped us to present this book to our English speaking patrons.

We are also grateful to all those authors whose books have been consulted or quoted, while compiling this book, specially Maulana Muhammad Yousuf Islahi, whose book 'Husn-e-Muashrat' has been greatly depended upon.

We hope this book will immensely help to build up the society — specially a Muslim society on sound footings and guide the parents and children at every stage to discharge their duties and obligations justly.

30th September 1979

Akhlaq Husain

Parental Rights

The biggest right over mankind is that of Almighty Allah. Faith in and obedience to Him are our first and foremost duties. After these are the responsibilities of domestic life. Fulfilment of these responsibilities by trying to correct and construct the domestic life is a social need as well as religious duty.

After this begins the family life in which parents are entitled to the highest place and foremost rights. This can be substantiated by going through the following verses from the Holy Quran:

> "Your Lord Allah has decreed that you worship none but Him and that you be kind to parents whether one or both of them attain old age in your life. Say not to them a word of contempt nor repel them but address them in terms of honour and out of kindness lower to them the wing of humility and say —"My Lord bestow on both of them Your mercy as they cherished me in my childhood. (17:23-24)

If we go through these verse for the Holy Quran repeatedly and ponder over them the following points will be evident:

(1) Parent's rights are next to those of Almighty Allah in Islam. This is authenticated by the fact that, after the description of the Unity of Almighty Allah, the Holy Quran has repeatedly ordered of the most pleasant and submissive behaviour with the parents.

Muslim Parents

(2) When parents become old their temperament is changed. They usually become easily irritable and short tempered due to their age. Their children should take these changes for granted and show considerable patience and magnanimity for their aging parents.

(3) Parents should be respected and revered throughout all the stages of their ages alike. Particularly when they are old and become persistent, nagging, critical etc; the children should all the more be submissive and tolerant and should always keep in mind the related verses from the Holy Book.

(4) The children should adopt attitudes of humbleness, politeness and obedience for the parents. They should readily carry out the orders of parents and also feel comforted by doing so. In old age when parents are invalid and naturally depend upon their children, the children should serve them like an obedient servant. While doing so, instead of showing or even feeling benevolence or pity, they should rather feel exalted and thank Almighty Allah for getting the opportunity of serving their parents in their old age.

(5) We should recall those days of infancy when we were totally dependent on our parents. During that period we were weak and in need of help from the parents to survive. In those days the parents nourished us with love and affection bearing all sorts of hardships. They felt happy when we were happy and became restless when we were even slightly harmed. The children should always have these memories fresh in mind and pray to Almighty Allah to be Merciful and Kind to their parents in their old age as they had been considerate and kind to them in their hour of need.

Parental Rights

The facts which are mentioned in the above quoted two verse from the Holy Quran are elaborated and practised upon by our Holy Prophets (S.A.W.).

Importance of Parents

> (1) Hazrat Abu Umamah narrated once a man asked the Holy Prophet (S.A.W.) about the rights of parents upon their children. He replied that "the parents are the Heaven or Hell for their children".
>
> (Ibn-e-Majah, Mishkat)

This saying of the Holy Prophet means that nobody can belittle the importance of parents. Leaving apart their importance in social life, one can clearly understand that from the point of view of deliverance in the life Hereafter, he can earn an abode in Heaven by keeping the parents happy. On the other hand he can be a deserving person for Hell if he makes them unhappy by his untoward behaviour.

(2) Hazat Abdullah Bin Amr narrates that the Holy Prophet said:

"The pleasure of Allah lies in the pleasure of father and the displeasure of Allah lies in the displeasure of father. (Tirmizi, Hakim)

Nobody can get the pleasure of Almighty Allah without pleasing the parents. One who earns the pleasure of the parents pleases Almighty Allah. One who displeases the parents can never be saved from His wrath. Both the things are interdependent.

Hazrat Moaviyah, sons of Hazrat Jahemah, once came to the Last Messenger of Almighty Allah and sought his advice about taking part in the Holy War (Jihad) with him. The Holy Prophet asked him whether his mother was alive? He answered in the affirmative. The Holy Prophet then told him. "Go back home and serve here as Heaven was under her feet." (Ibn-e-Majah, Nasai)

"Heaven was under her feet," is a very comprehensive sentence. It actually means that mother must be highly respected, treated with extreme politeness and submission and served selflessly by those who want deliverance on the Day of Judgement. In the first Hadith the importance of the obedience of father is shown while the other establishes the worth of obedience to mother.

> Hazrat Abu Hurairah narrates:- "The Holy Prophet cursed the person three times who found his parents whether or one old and he did not earn Heaven (by serving them)." (Muslim)

Worldly Reward of Serving the Parents

No other reward is greater than earning the pleasure of Almighty Allah and deserving the entrance to Heaven by serving and obeying the parents. This reward is to be enjoyed in the life Hereafter. But those who uphold the rights of their parents and serve them sincerely are also rewarded in their Worldly lives by Almighty Allah.

The Holy Prophet once told a very interesting anecdote to his companions about three persons. According to Him three persons were, once, travelling when heavy rains began to fall. They took shelter in a cave. Incidentally a big stone came hurtling down and blocked the opening of the cave. All the three travellers lost the hope of their survival. One of them told the rest not to lose hope and pray to Almighty Allah, by describing the most virtuous deed of their lives, for enabling them to get out of the cave which had not exit.

One of them addressing to Almighty Allah, submitted that he had old parents and several small children. When he would come back home after grazing the goats he would first offer the milk to his parents and then to his children. Once when he came home quite late his parents were asleep. He milked the goats as usual and taking the cup of milk went to his parents but could not dare to disturb their sleep. So he stood there the whole night holding the cup in his hands, ignoring the cries of his small children who clung to his feet to be fed. He did not like the very idea of feeding his children while his parents were sleeping with empty stomachs. He beseeched Almighty Allah to enable them to come out of the cave if He judged that the man did so to please Him. Suddenly the big stone slided a little from the mouth of the cave. Then the remaining two travellers too prayed to Almighty Allah by describing their own virtuous deeds each for His judgement. As they finished, the big stone slided completely from the opening of the cave and they were free to move out by the grace of Almighty Allah.

Nice Behaviour with Parents

Once Hazrat Abdullah-Bin Masood asked the Holy Prophet (S.A.W.) to tell him the deed liked most by Almighty Allah. The

Muslim Parents

Holy Prophet replied, "To offer prayers in time." He again asked him to tell the second best. He was told. "To behave nicely with the parents". Then Hazrat Abdullah asked about the third one and he was told by the Holy Prophet, "To take part in the Holy War (Jihad) in the way of Almighty Allah." (Bukhari and Muslim).

The importance of nice behaviour with parents can be judged by the fact that our Holy Prophet Muhammad (S.A.W.) has stressed upon it together with the most important duty of offering the prayers. (Salat). This implies the fact that we should not take it as a worldly affair only but should well understand that it is our religious duty too. Those who are disobedient to the parents are disobedient to Almighty Allah and His Holy Prophet, both have laid much emphasis on obeying, serving and pleasing the parents by their children. Those who are disobedient to the parents are disobedient to Almighty Allah and His Holy Prophet as well. They are committing a social crime as well as a sin against Almighty Allah who will punish them for this disgression.

Hazrat Abdullah, son of Hazrat Amr-Bin-Al'As, narrates that a person came to the Holy Prophet for accompanying him in emigration (Hijrah) and the Holy War (Jihad) to please Almighty Allah. The Holy Prophet enquired, "Is your father or mother alive?" One being replied by the man that both of them were alive the Prophet of Allah asked him whether he really wanted to earn reward from Almighty Allah for Hyrah and Jihad' He replied in the affirmative. Then the Holy Prophet said, "Go back to your parents and behave nicely with them. (Muslim).

Nobody can deny the importance of the Emigration and the Holy War (Jihad). But in case, the parents are aged, weak, ill or invalid it is more rewarding in the eyes of Islam to serve them remaining at home than embarking upon the emigration (Hijra) or participating in the Holy War (Jihad).

The same narrator relates that a person came to the Holy Prophet to take part in the Emigration (Hijrah) against the will of his weeping parents. The Holy Prophet told him to go back to his parents and come back only after pleasing them as he had made them cry. (Abu Dawood).

Respect and Reverence for Parents

Once Hazrat Abu Hurairah, one of the senior companions of the Holy Prophet, came across two persons. He asked one of them, about the other. The person replied that the other one was his respected father. Then Hazrat Abu Hurairah strictly advised the son never to call his father by the name and neither to walk ahead of him nor to take seat before he takes the seat first in a gathering. (Al-Adab Al-Mufrad).

Hazrat Taila Ibn Miyas narrates that once, while participating in a war, he was lured to commit some mistakes. He soon realized his mistake and became much worried. Getting an opportunity he referred the whole matter to Hazrat Abdullah-Bin Umar who asked about the facts. After hearing him, he replied, those were not the Major sins which were only nine in number—viz.

(1) Polytheism

(2) Homicide

(3) To flee from Jihad

(4) Slandering the pious women

(5) Taking or giving interest

(6) To usurp orphan's property

(7) Blasphemous conversation in the mosque

(8) To make mockery of Islam

(9) Disobedience to parents

Then he stated him whether he wished to go to Hell or keep off it. Hazrat Taila replied that by Almighty Allah he earnestly desired to go in Heaven. Hazrat Abdullah then asked him whether his parents were alive. He replied that only his mother was alive. Hazrat Abdullah then, swearing by Almighty Allah, assured him of earning an entry in Heaven if he talked to his mother with extreme politeness and served her extremely well. But he also warned him against committing the major sins.

Compensation for Parents

Hazrat Abu Hurairah stated that the Holy Prophet said: "The love, care and hardships (faced during up-bringing the children) of the parents could hardly be compensated if one gets his parents freed from slavery by paying their price on finding them in such a condition. (Muslim, Tirmizi, Abu Dawood).

Compensation for Mother

The same narrator states that once Hazrat Abdullah-Bin-Umar saw a Yemenite, circumambulating (Tawaf) Holy Kaba with his mother on his back, who was enthusiastically reciting the following verses:

"I am a camel acting on the impulses of the rider and when other (camels) become uncontrollable and run astray I do not."

Seeing Hazrat Abdullah he asked that had he not compensated for the rights of his mother? Hazrat Abdullah replied that it was not the compensation even for a single birth pang of his mother.

Conduct of Hazrat Abu Hurairah with his Mother

Once Marwan appointed Hazrat Abu Hurairah to officiate him for some days in his absence. At that time he was in Zul Hulaifah and his mother was living in another house at some distance from him. Whenever he went out he would first come to the house of his mother and say, "My dear mother, peace be upon you and may Allah be merciful to you." The mother would reply, "My dear son, peace be upon you too and may Allah be merciful to you." He again would say, "May Allah be kind to you as you have been kind to me in my childhood." She would reply, "My dear son, may Allah be kind to you as you are kind to me now in my old age." He would repeat it when he would come back home.

Climax of the Obedience to Parents

Hazrat Abdullah narrates that the Holy Prophet told a person that one who awoke in the morning as obedient to his parents according to the Commandments of Almighty Allah, was like one who found the two doors opened for him in Heaven. And he will find one door opened if any one of his parent was alive. But one who broke the day as disobedient to his parents contravening the commandments of Almighty Allah, was like one who found the two doors opened for him in Hell. And he will find one door opened if any one of his parents was alive. The man asked the Holy Prophet that should one be obedient to his parent even if they were callous to him? The Holy Prophet replied, "Yes, even if they are callous; yes, even if they are callous; yes, even if they are callous."

This Hadith also makes it clear that one should be obedient only to Almighty Allah and to nobody else. The obedience towards the parents is only necessary by virtue of the fact that it has been commanded by Almighty Allah. Momins (true Muslims) do not obey the parents who ask them to act against the Commandments of Almighty Allah.

To obey the parents even if they are callous towards their children means that should such parents, out of their harshness or short temper, make impossible and unreasonable demands, the children should continue serving them and behaving them nicely and patiently. Though in such a condition Almighty Allah does not make the children duty bound to obey such parents as He never burdens anybody beyond his capacity. But the climax of the obedience to the parents implies that the children should serve their parents and keep them pleased at all costs.

It is also to be clarified here that, with reference to the Hadith quoted earlier, it does not mean that if one of your parents is dead and you will have only one door opened for you in Heaven by being obedient to the remaining one. Rather it means that in case you are obedient to the one and otherwise to the other then you have one entrance to the heaven but at the same time you have also an entrance to Hell by disobeying the other one. This should keep both of them happy by his pleasant behaviour.

Parental Rights

When to Disobey the Parents

Despite the emphasis laid upon the obedience and gratitude for parents in social life there are certain situations in which one can, should and must disobey the parents. This has been stressed in the laws of Shariah. In Islam the obedience is basically a right of Almighty Allah. Besides Him others can only be obeyed if He has bestowed upon them this privilege. So, even the parents, can only be obeyed upto the limits prescribed by Islam.

Disobeying Almighty Allah by obeying the parents will only lead a Muslim towards earning His wrath. Obedience of parents according to the canons of Islam will no doubt please Him but doing so against His commandments will definitely displease Him.

A very famous Hadith, about the parent's rights, is narrated by Hazrat Abdullah-bin-Umar. According to him, he had a wife whom he loved fervently, but his father, the great Caliph 'Umar, disliked her. Ultimately Hazrat 'Umar asked him to divorce her, but he did not obey his pious father. Hazrat 'Umar, then, went to the Holy Prophet Muhammad (S.A.W.) and related all that to him. The Holy Prophet told Hazrat Abdullah, "Divorce her." (Abu Dawood, Tirmizi, Nasai, Ibn Majah)

No doubt this Hadith does call upon the children to obey their parents readily and not even imagine to do otherwise. But it does not, in any case, mean that the children should do so beyond its limitations. But the explicit wordings of this Hadith people get misconceived about its implicit meanings. They think the parents can rightly order their sons or daughters to divorce their spouses regardless of the fact that they are pious and faithful and in no case deserve such treatment which has no legal (Islamic) sanction. This is, totally, a misinterpretation.

This incident is related to the well-known Caliph-Hazrat 'Umar. How can we imagine, for a moment, that he was a cruel or a prejudicial person. He was one of the best interpreters of the Holy Quran and Hadith. Moreover he was also a man of justice and impartiality. He had ample knowledge about the rights of spouses. In the light of these facts we cannot even think for a moment that he asked his son to divorce his wife due to some personal grudge and dislike for his daughter-in-law.

Consequently one can only deduce the fact that there was some greater religious, ethical and social purpose before him when he insisted for this divorce. He did not do so, undoubtedly only for imposing his authority, as a father upon his son.

On the other hand Abdullah-Bin-Umar was himself a pious, true Muslim. He very well knew the demands of his religion and strictly followed Sunnah (practice of the Holy Prophet). Nevertheless when he was asked by his pious father to divorce his wife he refused to do so. He did so as he was not fully aware of the religious, ethical and social justifications of this demand which were no doubt foreseen by his father. But Hazrat 'Umar did not rebuke his son for his disobedience. Rather he brought the case to the Holy Prophet for decision—last and final. The Holy Prophet, after due consideration, agreed with Hazrat 'Umar and asked Hazrat Abdullah to divorce his wife.

It goes without saying that the Holy Prophet would never have agreed with Hazrat 'Umar without giving due consideration

Parental Rights

to and being satisfied with the justness of the reasons given by Hazrat 'Umar for the divorce.

Consequently we come to the conclusion that the children are not bound to obey the seemingly untoward orders of their parents unless they are not absolutely convinced by the exactness and intensity of the reasons given for those commands. But here a word of caution seems necessary. The children, in such situations, must give serious consideration to the orders of their parents instead of outright refusal, because, being their true well-wishers, the parents may be right.

Advice of Hazrat Abu Darda

This interpretation of the Hadith under discussion is supported by still another Hadith quoted by Hazrat Abu Darda.

A man came to him and said that, insistingly, his father made him marry a girl but now asks him to divorce her. Hazrat Abu Darda replied that neither he could advice him to disobey his parents nor to divorce his wife. But he would only tell him that once he heard the Holy Prophet of Almighty Allah saying,

"A father is the best door to Heaven. So it is upto you to either get it reserved for you or leave it." (Ibn Habban)

The most considerable point in this Hadith is that although the man made it crystal clear that his father was ordering him to divorce his wife but Hazrat Abu Darda didnot advise him to blindly obey his father. Instead he abstained himself from favouring or disfavouring the issue. If the obedience of parents would have been unconditional, he would have definitely

Muslim Parents

counselled the man to divorce his wife. So, acting judiciously, he told him the Hadith for making him think and decide himself about the issue while avoiding injustice to the parents as they had the key to Heaven for their children.

Acts Beneficial For The Parents After Their Death

Hazrat Abu Osaid narrated that once, while he was sitting with the Holy Prophet, someone asked him whether there were any steps which he could take to benefit his parents even after their death. He replied, "Yes" there are four such things (1) to pray for their deliverance and forgiveness, (2) to accomplish their promises and carry out their (proper) wills, (3) to respect and treat their friends well, (4) and to be nice and kind to those who are related to you through your parents." (Al-Adab Al— Mufrad)

In fact the hardships borne and services rendered by the parents during the upbringing and training of their children can never be repaid even if the children serve them like slaves. This is why that the true Muslims serve their parents sincerely and devotedly till the end of their lives. But after their death they still have the uneasy feeling of not having served them well. Consequently they continue searching the way and means through which they could benefit the departed souls of their dear parents and thus earn their own satisfaction too.

For this purpose the Holy Prophet Muhammad (S.A.W.) pointed out towards four measures to be adopted by the children.

1. Prayer for Deliverance

After each prescribed prayer (salat) and at other appropriate occasions one should invocate for the forgiveness of the sins and deliverance of his parents to Almighty Allah. He should also pray that may Almighty Allah bestow upon them all what He bestows upon His pious slaves.

According to Hazrat Abu Hurairah, the Prophet of Almighty Allah once said that when a person died, his period of activity was over. But there were three things which remain benefiting him even after his death.

(1) Lasting acts of welfare (Sadaqah Jariah)
(2) His knowledge beneficial for the people
(3) His pious children who prayed for his deliverance.

Hazrat Ibn-i-Sereen, a pious Muslim scholar, narrated that once Hazrat Abu Hurairah prayed to Almighty Allah, may the sins of Abu Hurairah be forgiven, May the sins of Abu Hurairah's mother be forgiven and may the sins of those be forgiven who pray for the forgiveness of the sins of Abu Hurairah and his mother. Hazrat Ibn Sereen said that he and all others who were present there continued praying for the deliverance of Hazrat Abu Hurairah and his mother in order to get the benefit of Hazrat Abu Hurairah's prayer for themselves too.

2. Fulfillment of Commitments and Wills of Parents

If the children come to know about some unfulfilled commitments made by their parents to others during their lifetime and about their will at the time of their death, they should try their best to fulfill those commitments and will in order to get the souls of their parents benefitted. But while doing so the children should take care that they are fulfilling only the just and proper commitments and will otherwise they will be harming them as well as their own-selves.

Acts Beneficial For The Parents After Their Death

Hazrat Abdullah-bin-Abbas related that a man came to the Holy Prophet and told that his mother had died without making her will. He, then asked that could the soul of his departed mother be benefitted if he gave something away to the deserving in the name of Almighty Allah. The Holy Prophet replied, "Yes, Yes, Why not?

Hazrat Abdullah further narrated that Hazrat Sad-bin-Ubadah told the Holy Prophet that his mother died before fulfilling the vows which she had promised. Could he fulfill that vow on her behalf? The beloved Prophet replied, "Why not? Fulfil it for her."

3 Pleasant Behaviour with the Persons close to the Parents

The third measure to be taken by the children in this direction is to be nice and respectful towards the near and dear ones to their parents. They should be respected like ones own parents. Their opinions and their counsels should be given due importance and they should always be treated well.

Once the Holy Prophet proclaimed, "The most commendable behaviour of a person is to treat the friends and acquaintances of his father kindly."

Behaviour of the Pious Companions of the Holy Prophet

Once Hazrat Abu Darda fell critically ill. Knowing this Hazrat Yousuf-bin-Abdullah came to enquire about his health, covering a considerably long distance. Hazrat Abu Darda was surprised to see him there and asked, "How did you come here?"

Muslim Parents

Hazrat Yousuf replied, "Sir, I came here only to enquire about your health for, my respected father had most friendly relations with you."

Hazrat Abdullah-bin-Umar once met a bedouin on his way to Mecca. The bedouin looked minutely at him and asked that whether he was the son of Hazrat Umar. Hazrat Abdullah, replying in the affirmative, gave his turban to the bedouin and made him sit respectfully on his own donkey. According to Hazrat Ibn Dinar who was one of the co-travellers, all of us were surprised to see it. They asked Hazrat Abdullah the reason for giving so much respect to a bedouin. He replied that the bedouin's father was a friend of Hazrat Umar and then quoted the Holy Prophet, "Maintain the friendship of your father and do not let it be finished otherwise Almighty Allah will put off the light (Noor) for you".

Hazrat Abu Bardah relates that when he went to Madina, Hazrat Abdullah Ibn 'Umar came to him. He asked Hazrat Abu Bardah whether he knew the purpose of his visit. He replied in the negative. Hazrat Abdullah then told him that he had heard the last Prophet of Almighty Allah saying that 'one who wanted his father to be benefitted in his grave, should behave kindly with the friends and acquaintances of his deceased father.' Hazrat Abdullah said, their fathers were intimate friends and I want to preserve and keep that friendship alive. (Ibn Habban).

4. The fourth in which the parents can be benefitted after their death is to treat their relatives with kindness. It means that the children should be kind and nice towards their both paternal and maternal aunts, uncles grandfathers and grandmothers. If they are unkind to them they are unkind to their own parents.

Acts Beneficial For The Parents After Their Death

The Holy Prophet has advised the Muslims, "Never neglect your ancestors. Neglecting the parents means ungratefulness to Almighty Allah."

Fruits of Praying for the Deliverance of Parents

"Hazrat Anas related that once the Holy Prophet said, "If a slave of Almighty Allah always remained disobedient to his parents and if they both or none of them died during such a condition, he should continuously pray for the deliverance of his parents. He should go on doing so till Almighty Allah includes him in the category of the virtuous persons."

In fact the children should continue obeying their parents throughout their whole lives to keep them happy. But in case they remain displeased with them despite their best efforts and die in this condition, they should still continue their efforts in this direction. They should keep praying for their deliverance so that Almighty Allah may forgive their faults of not keeping their parents pleased with them. And thus Almighty Allah may be pleased to award them deliverance too.

Looking at the Parents with Love and Affection

Hazrat Ibn Abbas narrates the saying of the Holy Prophet, "The virtuous children who once look at their parents with love, Almighty Allah gives them the benefit of one accepted Hajj." Somebody asked, "O, Prophet of Allah if one looks hundred times like this at his parent in a day?" He replied, "Yes, Allah is Far Greater (than you can imagine) and infallible."

It means that nobody can estimate the scope of the Grace and Mercy of Almighty Allah. One will think that the above mentioned reward of casting one affectionate glance at the parents by their children is more than sufficient. But He is so limitlessly bountiful as to increase this reward to hundred times if the children do so for hundred times. And it is beyond human imagination to measure the scope of His bounties.

Financial help to the Parents

Almighty Allah says,

"They ask you {O'Messenger} what they should spend. Say whatever of good you spend let it be for the parents..."

(2:215)

Apart from service, submission and obedience to the parents the Holy Quran and Sunnah have also stressed upon the children not to be miserly towards them; rather they should give first preference to their parents in spending their money. They are even entitled to take money from their children by compulsion in their hour of need. It is absolutely unfair of the children to keep their money off parents even if they are always obedient to them. Because obedience to the parents includes their financial help also.

Right of Father in the Wealth of his Son

Once a man complained to the Holy Prophet about his father who took away his belongings whenever he liked. The Last Messenger of Allah called for his father, who was a very old man, and asked him the details of the matter. He said. "O' Messenger of Allah, a time was when he (the son) was weak and helpless and barehanded while I had strength and wealth. I never hesitated to give him my belongings whenever he needed

Acts Beneficial For The Parents After Their Death

them. Today I am weak and barehanded while he is rich and now he keeps his belongings off me." Hearing this tears came to the eyes of the Holy Prophet, then he said to the son,

> "You and your belongings belong to your father. You and your belongings belong to your father."

The Debts of Parents

Hazrat Abdullah bin Zubair never neglected the rights of his parents even after they were dead. Hazrat Zubair was an affluent man. Usually as soon as any such person dies his children start clamouring for their shares from the belongings of the deceased. But Hazrat Abdullah was not at all worried about this when his rich father passed away. He could have been well anxious to get his share which amounted to crores, but his only anxiety was about the debts of his father which he wanted to repay without any exception.

Consequently he first cleared the debts of his father from the left property. Immediately the heirs started scolding him for getting their shares from the property of the deceased. But Hazrat Abdullah strictly told them to wait for four years. During these years, he said, he will announce on the occasion of Hajj to the people to come and collect their debts if any is due upon his departed father till not a single debt remains unpaid. Only after that he would distribute the property.

Virtues of Serving the Parents

Hazrat Anas bin Malik quotes the Holy Prophet to have once said.

Muslim Parents

"One who wants a long life and a sufficient sustenance should be good and kind to his parents and kinsmen."

This world is a place, for Muslims, where they should do best to earn the blessings of Almighty Allah and to make their Afterlife a successful. Getting longevity and being well off in token of one's devoted service to parents are no doubt the valuable rewards for him from Almighty Allah. It offers him an opportunity as well as facility to add to his good deeds and prove himself worthy of the bounties of the Creator. According to Hazrat Moaz bin Anas, the Last Messenger of Almighty Allah (S.A.W.) once said:

"There is good news for them who behaved well with their parents — Allah will increase the period of their lives."

Difference Between The Rights of Parents

Both the parents play their parts in bringing up the children at the cost of their own comforts and pleasures. The father feels happy to spend his hard earned money upon them while the mother feeds them from her own blood (milk). Thus the children are brought up by the joint toil, love and affection of both their parents. Consequently the best treatment from the children is stressed in the Holy Quran and Sunnah for them.

But it is also a bare fact that a mother makes more sacrifices and endures greater hardships than a father while bringing up the children. She feeds them and takes care of them by sacrificing her comforts in the day and her sleep in the night without any greed or compulsion but only out of sheer love and affection. Such a selfless and sincere love is unprecedented in human history. This is the reason why the Holy Quran has given more importance to the mother and stressed upon the children to be more considerate and submissive to her in comparison with the father.

According to the Holy Quran.
"And we have enjoined on man goodness to his parents. His mother bore him with pains and she delivered him with pain. And bearing him and weaning him is thirty months." (46 : 15)

At another place in the Holy Quran it is said;

"And we have stressed upon the man concerning his parents, whom his mother bore with pain after pain and his weaning is in two years, so thank Me and thy parents." (31 : 14)

Thus the fact comes to light that the mother deserves service, love, submission, obedience and gratitude from the children more than the father. This is justified because she faces acute hardships and makes unique sacrifices in bringing up her children.

A Thought Provoking Dialogue

A person came to the Holy Prophet (S.A.W.) and complained that his mother was ill-tempered. The Holy Messenger of Almighty Allah said:

"She was not ill tempered when she kept you in her womb for nine months." The person insisted, "Sir, I am telling you the truth that she is ill-tempered." The Holy Prophet said, "She was not ill-tempered when she used to keep awake the whole night for your sake and feed you". "I have recompensed all these favours of my mother", boasted the complainant. The Prophet, then asked, "How you have recompensed her?" "I have helped her perform Hajj by putting her on my shoulders." He replied. The Holy Prophet put a deciding and unanswerable question to the complainant, " Can you also recompense the painful pangs which your mother bore at the time of your birth?"

Hazrat Abu Hurairah relates that once a person came to the Holy Prophet (S.A.W.) and asked, "O Holy Messenger of

Difference Between The Rights of Parents

Allah who is the most deserving person to get nice treatment from me?" He replied, "Your mother ," He asked "Who next? To this he got the same reply. When he repeated this question for the fourth time, he was told by the Holy Prophet, "Your father." (Bukhari, Muslim)

This Hadis clearly proves that the status of mother is far greater than that of the father. Hazrat Ibne Battal proves it in a very logical manner. According to him, "The right of mother to be served and treated nicely is three times greater than that of the father for she renders three such services to her children which cannot even be imagined by the father. The mother bears the burden of the child during the period of pregnancy, stands the pains of delivery, and then feeds the child from her breasts." These three important services are also mentioned in the Holy Quran. As afterwards both father and mother play equal parts in training and bringing up the children, emphasis has been laid on the fair treatment for both of them by their children.

Though majority of religious scholars are agreed that mother enjoys greater rights than the father but in the least it did not mean that the children should serve the mother and ignore the father. As far as the respect and reverence is concerned, father is more deserving for these and negligence towards the father does not behave a true Muslim. For both of them nice behaviour is emphasised. But it should be borne in mind that mother is comparatively weaker in our society, and due to the greater services rendered by her she is more deserving to be comforted and treated nicely by the children.

Consideration For The Maternal Affection

In the days of the Holy Prophet (S.A.W.) one of his companions divorced his wife and wanted to take away the child from her too. She was doubly shocked. On the one hand she lost her husband and also feared the loss of her only child on the other. Frustrated and grief-striken she came to the Holy Prophet and told him her pathetic story in the follwing words:

'O' Messenger of Allah! My husband divorced me and I am deprived of his patronage. Now he wants to take away my little child from me too. O' Messenger of Allah! This is my beloved child. My belly is his bed, my breast is his feeding reservoir and my lap is his abode I am comforted by him. He brings water for me from the well. O' Messenger of Allah! How can I bear this shock?" The beloved Prophet told her to get the matter decided by a draw. Then the father came forward and said, "O Messenger of Allah! This is my child and who else can claim him but me." The Holy Prophet then said to the child, "This is your father and this is your mother, hold the hand of one whom like." The boy held the hand of his mother. He then told the mother, "Go home, nobody can take the child away from you till you marry again."

Carrying Out The Wishes of Mother

In the days of Hazrat Usman, one of the four pious caliphs and companion of the Holy Prophet (S.A.W.), the price of dates shot up. During that period people saw Hazrat Usman-bin-Zaid extracting the juice from a date tree by incising the tree with a knife. The people surprisingly asked that why was he destroying

Difference Between The Rights of Parents

the tree which was so costly in those days. He replied that he was doing so to carry out the wish of his mother who had asked him to bring the juice for her. "How can I ignore the desire of my mother?"

Nice Behaviour With Mother

A person came to the Holy Prophet and said. "O Messenger of Allah! I have committed a great sin. Is there any way for its atonement?" He asked the person whether his mother was alive. After getting the answer in the negative he again asked whether his maternal aunt was alive. Finding the reply in the affirmative he advised, "Then be nice to your maternal aunt."

We can well estimate by this anecdote the importance of nice behaviour with mother which can be a source of expiation of even the great sins. This shows the extreme beneficence of Almighty Allah that He has given us an opportunity to expiate our sins and be successful in our lives Hereafter by behaving nicely even with our maternal aunts in case the mother is dead.

Behaviour With The Foster Mother

Hazrat Abu-Tufail narrates that once when the Holy Prophet was distributing meat at Jaranah, a woman came very close to him. He spread his sheet for her - she sat on it. I asked the people about her. They told me that she was the foster mother of the Holy Prophet (S.A.W.). (Abu Dawood).

A women who feeds someone else's child on her own milk, is called his foster mother. Though by doing so, such a woman does not become a real mother but in some respects she enjoys the same status. As regard the matters of marriage and seclusion, Islam has not differentiated between the two. The above mentioned incident of the Holy Prophet also teaches us to behave with the foster mother just like the real mother.

Behaviour With The Non-Muslim Parents

In this world where the virtues and vices are always at war with each other, there is a possibility that the parents, of Muslim children may be non-Muslims. In such a situation how the children should behave with these parents? This is a pertinent question to be asked and answered in our social life. As far as faith and religion are concerned the Holy Quran has given the clear and final verdict. According to it, if parents force the children to abandon Islam they are forbidden to obey them. Of course, Almighty Allah enjoys more rights than the parents over the believers. It becomes necessary for the parents also to recognise this fact and they should obey Him and for He is their Creator and Master too. Obeying the parents and disobeying the Creator should not even be imagined by the true Muslim.

According to the Holy Quran,

> "But if they (parents) strive to make thee join with Me that of which thou hast no knowledge then obey them not." (29:8)

Not only obedience in ascribing partners to Almighty Allah is forbidden, but in any matter in which disobedience to Him is involved, the obedience to parents comes to an end. The Messenger of Almighty Allah (S.A.W.) has made it crystal clear that none could be obeyed in the disobedience of Almighty Allah.

Muslim Parents

The Infidel Mother of Hazrat S'ad

Hazrat S'ad-bin Waqqas was a prominent companion of the Holy Prophet. He embraced Islam at the age of nineteen. When his mother came to know about it, she swore that she would neither eat nor drink unless her son left Islam. Hazrat S'ad loved his mother very much. He was pained to see her pathetic condition but could not help her as this was a matter of faith. His mother repeatedly pleaded him that his religion has strongly stressed upon obeying the parents but he was not obeying his own mother. Thus, accordingly to her, he was negating his own religion. For three days she neither ate nor drank and ultimately became unconscious. His brother fed her forcibly by opening her mouth. On this occasion Almigty Allah revealed the above quoted verse.

In the matters against religion (Islam) they should definitely be disobeyed. Their pressure, force and displeasure should not be given any importance. But regarding other worldly affairs they should be readily obeyed, selflessly served and very nicely treated to induce them for embracing Islam which bestows them overriding importance.

Almighty Allah commands in the Holy Quran.

"And consort kindly with them in the world, and follow the path of him who turns unto Me." (31 : 15)

Islam has touched the extremes of obedience to parents as it commands the children to obey their infidel parents in all the matters except faith and religion. Even if they are infidel they are the parents and have given birth to them and have cherished them bearing the same pains and hardships which are faced by

Behaviour With The Non-Muslim Parents

the Muslim parents. Consequently, inspite of the religious differences, it is the duty of their Muslim children to serve and treat them with kindness, respect and devotion. They should also be helped financially and should not be given a chance to complain in worldly affairs.

The Hadis About The Infidel Mother

Hazrat Asma, daughter of Hazrat Abu Bakr (R.A.A.) narrates that once infidel mother visited her. She asked the Holy Prophet, 'My mother has come to me. She hates my religion. Can I behave her nicely?' He told her, "Yes, be kind to your mother."

This Hadis clearly suggests that the infidel parents should be treated as nicely as the Muslim ones. The children should not shirk from obeying, respecting and serving them in the affairs other than the faith.

Benefits of The Nice Behaviour with Infidel Mother

While Hazrat Abu Hurairah embraced Islam, his mother continued to be infidel for quite a long time. He continuously tried to convince her in favour of Islam but of no avail. Nevertheless, he continued respecting and obeying her. Once when he was trying to convince her she became insolent and uttered some insulting remarks about the Holy Prophet. Hazrat Abu Hurairah was very much pained. He went to the Holy Prophet and complained, "O Messenger of Allah! I have always been trying to make my mother accept Islam but she always refuses to accept it. But today when I asked her to believe in Almighty Allah, she became very much annoyed and started insulting and rebuking you which I could not stand and tears came to my eyes. O' Messenger of Allah! pray to Allah that may He open the heart of my dear mother for Islam." The Holy Prophet immediately raised his hands and prayed, "O' Almighty Allah! guide the mother of Abu Hurairah."

Hazrat Abu Hurairah was overjoyed and came back. When he reached home he found the door was bolted from inside but he heard the sound of flowing water, which assured him that his mother was taking a bath. Hearing his footsteps, she hastily finished the bath. Then she opened the door. She said, 'O my son Abu Hurairah, Allah has heard you. Be witness that I recite the Kalimah." He started crying out of sheer joy and went back to the Holy Prophet with the tiding that Almighty Allah had accepted his prayer and his mother had gotten the treasure of Islam. The Holy Prophet was also pleased to hear that. He praised Almighty Allah and gave him some advices. Then, on his request, he prayed, "O' Allah put the love of Abu Hurairah and his mother in the hearts of all true Muslims and put the love of all true Muslims in the hearts of both of them." According to Hazrat Abu Hurairah everyone, after that prayer, who saw him or heard about him, loved him.

Disobedience To Parents

After polytheism, the gravest sin is the disobedience to parents. This is an evil which a true Muslim cannot even imagine without repulsion. Thankfulness, gentleness and gratitude are the three basic qualities which make a man perfect. One who does not cultivate these basic attitudes in him cannot be called a human being. Such a person cannot be favoured by Almighty Allah as he can neither fulfil his duties towards Him nor the people: Hence Muslims who are obedient to Almighty Allah can never be disobedient or even careless to their parents.

The Worst Sin

Hazrat Abu Bakrah (Nafei-bin-Haris) narrates that once the Holy Prophet asked that should he not warn them against the three major sins? All of them said, certainly; O' Prophet! He, then said, "To ascribe partners with Allah, to disobey the parents. Getting up, as he was reclining, he said. "to tell a lie or to give false evidence." He went on repeating his words for such a long time that we wished him to be silent. (Bukhari, Muslim, Tirmizi).

In this Hadith the word "aqooq" has been used, for the disobedience to parents. It means carelessness, cruelty, painful attitude and disobedience.

The Letter of The Holy Prophet To The Yemenites

In a most important letter sent to the Yemenites through Amr-bin-Hazm the Holy Prophet warned them of the following sins:

Muslim Parents

1. To ascribe the partners with Allah.
2. To kill a believer without any justification.
3. To flee from Jihad (Holy War in the Way of Allah).
4. To disobey the parents.
5. To blemish the character of pious women.
6. To learn magic.
7. To take interest.
8. To usurp the belongings of the orphans.

Advice of The Holy Prophet

Hazrat Muaz-bin-Jabal was a prominent companion of the Holy Prophet. Hazrat Umar used to say that without "Muaz" his destruction was certain. Hazrat Muaz was often advised by the Last Messenger of Almighty Allah. Once the Holy Prophet advised him. "You should never ascribe the partners with Allah even if you are murdered or burnt alive. And never disobey your parents even if they order you to keep off your money or your family."

Abusing The Parents

Hazrat Abdullah-bin-Amr quotes the Holy Prophet to have once said, "To abuse the parents is also one of the major sins." The listeners (surprisingly) said, "O Messenger of Allah! can one abuse his own parents? "He replied" Yes, when one abuses the father of the other, in turn the other abuses his father. He calls bad names to other's mother, in turn the other calls bad names to his mother."

(Muslim, Bukhari, Tirmizi)

Disobedience To Parents

This means that abusing the parents of others is like abusing one's own parents. One should not abuse even the parents of others so that his parents may not be abused.

Rebuking The Parents

According to Hazrat Abu Tufail someone asked Hazrat Ali, whether the Holy Prophet had told him something which he had not told to anyone else. Hazrat Ali replied, "None except a writing which is kept in the scabbard of my sword." He then took our the writing from the sheath which reads, "May Allah curse him, who slaughters in the name of others but His, may Allah curse him who changes the land boundries, may Allah curse him who curses his parents, and may Allah curse him who introduces innovations in the religion (Islam)."

Parents, after all, are human beings and susceptible to weaknesses and desires. It is possible that they might say or do something wrong and offending to the children. In such circumstances the children should not mind the acts or utterances of their parents. They should not become enraged at such things and start rebuking or cursing them. Whatever the parents may do to the children, they should control their temper keeping in view the hardships and ordeals stood by their parents in the course of their cherishment.

No doubt the parents, by their unjust behaviour, can create certain situations in which the children may become rebellious and disobedient to them. Especially when the father remarries and the children have to live with their step-mother who is usually callous and uncompromising with them. It is often seen that the step-mother tries to get her husband sore towards his children.

In most of the cases the fathers - out of love and consideration for their new brides, do change their attitude towards their children, ad maltreat them. They too become like step-fathers to their own children. Similarly if the mother marries again after divorce or death of her husband, the second husband does not like that his wife treat her and his children alike. And the poor wife, in order to please her husband, is compelled to adopt a different attitude towards her and husband's children.

In such cases the parents are justly to be blamed. It is the duty of the relatives and other concerned persons to make such parents realize their fault and remember their duty. They should compel them, through family and social pressures, to treat their children properly. At the same time the children should control their emotions in such circumstances. They should continue respecting their parents and avoiding any untoward behaviour with them as they are duty-bound to respect and obey their parents.

Ready Punishment For Disobeying The Parents

Hazrat Abu Bakrah (Nafei-bin-Haris) narrates that the Holy Prophet said, "Allah postpones the punishment for one's sins till the day of Judgement if He so desires. But He awards the punishment for disobeying the parents during this life, before his death.

It means that the disobedient children wil be punished twice—once in this world and secondly in After life.

Nullifying The Virtues

Hazrat Sauban narrates the Holy Prophet said:

Disobedience To Parents

"There are three sins which nullify all other virtues.

(1) Ascribing partners with Allah,
(2) disobedience to parents,
(3) and fleeing from Jihad."

Disobedience To Mother

Hazrat Abu Isa Mughairah bin Shubah relates that the Holy Prophet once said, "Be sure that Allah has forbidden you to disobey mother, to be miserly and greedy, and to bury the (new born) daughters alive. And He dislikes you to be talkative and too inquisitive and to waste your belongings."

It also implies that we should take extreme care of the sentiments, habits temperament and likes and dislikes of mother. We should not even imagine to be rude and disobedient to her. By serving and obeying our mother we can be sure of earning the favour of Almighty Allah.

Our success lies in our fair treatment with the parents, so that they remain happy with us and pray for our good and betterment. Failure and misfortune befalls on us when they curse us, being pained and unhappy by our behaviour.

The last Messenger of Allah says:

"There are three prayers which will, no doubt, be granted by Almighty Allah—

(1) Prayers of the oppressed
(2) prayers of a traveller and
(3) prayers of parents for their children.

Muslim Parents

The extent of suffering resulting from disobedience to mother can be assessed by the following anecdote:

Once, when the Holy Prophet was talking to his companions a man came and addressed him, "O' Messenger of Allah! A young man is breathing his last. People are asking him to recite Kalimah but he is unable to do so." The Holy Prophet asked, "Did this man offer prayers," and got the answer in the affirmative. Then he accompanied the man to the house of the dying young man alongwith others present at the time. The man was at the end of his life journey. The Messenger of Allah advised him to offer Kalimah. The man replied that he was unable to do so as the words did not come out of his mouth. He then called for the mother of the dying man whom he had disobeyed persistently. When his aged mother approached the scene, the Holy Prophet asked, "Respected lady, is he your son?" She replied in the affirmative. He then put her a question, "O respected lady, if we threaten to throw your son in a raging fire, will you recommend him to be forgiven?" The Lady replied that she would definitely do so at that time. The Holy Prophet then said to her, "If so, declare, making Allah and me your witnesses, that you are now pleased with him." The old woman readily declared, "O' Allah you and your Messenger be my witness that I am pleased with this beloved son of mine."

Just after that the Holy Prophet turned to the dying man and asked him to recite, "There is no god but Allah. He is One and has no partners and I witness that Muhammad is His Servant and His Messenger." By the virtue of the forgiveness of his mother he found the words flowing out of his mouth and he recited the Kalimah.

Disobedience To Parents

Seeing this the Holy Prophet praised Almighty Allah and thanked Him saying. "Thanks to Almighty Allah that He saved this man from the fearful fire of Hell through me."

(Tabarani, Ahmad)

Reward For Nice Treatment With The Parents—At A Glance

1. The biggest blessing of Almighty Allah for the Muslims is their parents. After the Creator, parents are the only ones who look after their children. Thus if the children are not grateful to their parents they shall be deemed as ungrateful to Almighty Allah also. Gratitude for parents is not at all different from gratitude for Him.

2. If one pleases his parents he positively pleases Almighty Allah too. One can earn His pleasure or wrath by pleasing or displeasing his parents respectively.

3. Nice treatment with parents and serving them devotedly is equivalent to the virtuous deed of Jihad and even greater than this in certain situations. By serving them one will enjoy the blessed status of a Mujahid (one who fights in the way of Allah).

4. One who earns the pleasure of his parents will surely be delievered on the Day of Judgement.

5. Children who have the opportunity of serving their parents are no doubt the lucky ones. By serving them you will entitle yourself for paradise, by neglecting them you will destroy your future life.

Muslim Parents

6. Performing Hajj and Umrah are the most virtuous deeds. But, if the children treat their parents nicely, Almighty Allah will bestow upon them the same reward.

7. Service of parents relieves a person from sufferings and calamities. If you treat them well, it is hoped Allah will forgive your sins.

8. Allah blesses and increases the age and livelihood of those who are obedient and submissive to their parents.

Rights of Children

Longing For Children

Everybody longs to have children to make a home pleasant and happy. Without them a home looks desolate and joyless. The long for children is quite natural. Almighty Allah has made it so to make this world survive. Otherwise how this world would have proliferated? Consequently He had put it in the very nature of men and women to long for children.

Particularly a woman has a greater urge for children. After getting married she anxiously waits to become a mother. She feels elated to bear children and endures the terrible pains of childbirth. She certainly knows that this ordeal might be fatal for her and even then she wants to have children. When she casts a glance at a new-born child lying beside her, she forgets all her worries and pains and is absorbed in his service. She goes on bearing all sorts of pains and hardships for them throughout her life.

Specially a Muslim woman bears all these pains and hardships for her children as her religious duty. According to Islam this world is not an end in itself, rather it is a means of achieving the sublime aim of deliverance by one's virtuous deeds. Apart from being benefited by fulfilling duties in this world, a Muslim will also be rewarded by Almighty Allah in the life Hereafter. So a Muslim mother who obeys the commandments of Almighty Allah regarding the cherishment of children will get the bounties of Allah here and Hereafter both. That is why she all the more bears and cherishes her children readily, selflessly and devotedly.

Islam provides the best chances of satisfaction to its followers. If one does not get any reward or benefit for the fulfilment of his duties in this world, he has a firm belief that he would be rewarded in the life Hereafter. And that will be a reward ample and ever lasting. Due to this conviction the Muslim mother continues fulfilling her duties towards the children even if she is not getting its expected results. According to Hadis:

When a woman is pregnant she enjoys, for the whole period of her pregnancy, the status of a person who keeps fasts, prays during most of the night, obeys Allah and fights for Him. And none can estimate the reward she earns from Allah for the pains she endures while delivering the child. And when he is born and she feeds the baby her milk she gets, for each sip of the milk, the reward like one who gives life to somebody. And when (after the specified period) she weans the child the angel of Allah putting his hand on her shoulder with respect and affection, says to her, "O' (maid of Allah) now be prepared for the next pregnancy."

(Kanz-Al-Ummal).

Expectations of Parents

Parents who bring up their children with such unique sacrifices naturally have certain expectations from them. They want them to be successful, obedient and devoted, in accordance with their own thinking and attitudes, and upholders of their own religious and cultural values. And when their dreams come true,

Rights of Children

when they see their children treading the path of their choice, and when they find them reaching at the climax of greatness and piety, there is no instrument yet invented to gauge their pride and pleasure. It is only and only the parents who wish to see their children surpass them in every field of life.

Grievances of Parents In General

Who can imagine the grief and disappointment of parents if their children, whom they have brought up and cherished with unparalleled patience and sacrifices, start behaving insolently and rebelliously with them?

Now-a-days, barring few lucky families, parents are generally seen complaining about the head-strongness and disobedience of their children. Their hearts bleed over the totally unexpected and untoward attitude of their children towards them. According to them their sons and daughters are no longer dutiful, submissive, considerate and respectful towards them and it seems as if they do not know these things at all.

Particularly the elderly people all the more complain about such things. They are much pained by such radical changes which have occurred in this direction. Whenever they get a chance they occurred their good old days when children could not even dare to speak loudly before their parents. Then they will start grumbling about the "stagnating society, immoral standard of education, and fashionable style of life, with uncessable contempt and favour for hours. And keeping in view such social and moral changes in values which are (as they think) beyond their control, the parents console themselves thinking that they are absolutely unable to do anything in these circumstances. They can only be the silent spectators, though boiling from within, to what is happening around them. Because, if they say or do anything against the prevailing conditions regarding the current attitudes and behaviour of young children, they will all the more lose their remaining status by this confrontation, enough to make the children more critical and disdainful towards them.

This is of course, a very sad state of affairs. This tussle between the parents and their children, in several cases, takes a very heavy toll in the shape of the disintegration of a happy family. So how can we remain unconcerned and let this condition gain more disastrous proportions? This has now become a universal social problem and everywhere, thinkers, scholars, social workers and sociologists are trying their best to alleviate this disastrous problem of strained parent-child relationship.

What The Parents Should Do

Parents play the most important role in shaping the personalities of their children. There are no two opinions about this. This is a universally acclaimed and agreed fact. In view of the problems mentioned above, it is the moral and religious duty of the parents to assess their own behaviour with the children. They should analyse and see whether they are sincerely fulfilling the duties assigned to them by Almighty Allah for their children or otherwise. This is a matter of natural give and take. If the parents have treated their children with care, love and affection, how can they expect their children to behave them nicely? If the parents have not taught them to respect and love the parents as their moral and religious duties, they have no right to even think that the children will be respectful and kind to them. Parents

Rights of Children

who have always preferred their own comfort and pleasure than those of their children, are living in a fools paradise if they expect their children to love them. The children of such parents grow with a sense of insecurity which plays havoc with their personality and ultimately make them wayward, rebellious and particularly disrespectful and insolent towards the parents.

Parents are much pained when they are disobeyed and disrespected by their children. They grumble that the children, who they have nursed and nurtured with pain and hardships, have now no regard for their old age and do not care for their requirements. But if they analyse and go deep to find out the hidden elements for this behaviour of their children, they will find only themselves to be blamed for such a state of affairs. They will find out that whatever they did for the upbringing of their children, they did it as an unpleasant burden which was thrust upon them against their wishes. They have always been wishing them to be dead as they were undergoing difficulties and hardships for them. Whenever possible, they made their ownselves easy and comforted neglecting and overlooking the comfort of their children. They fulfilled their own needs without giving any importance to the needs of their children.

There is another category of such parents who no doubt faced extreme hardships and difficulties in upbringing their children. They did sacrifice their own comforts and pleasures and kept their children comforted and happy to the best of their means. But unfortunately with all this and more, they did not care to teach their children about their duties towards them in the early stages of their childhood and adolescence. They did not inculcate in the minds of their children the basic attitudes of

Muslim Parents

love, respect, submission, devotion and obedience towards the parents and others concerned. They forgot to imprint upon their minds even the basic teachings of Islam about their duties towards the parents and the rest of the society in which they will have to live till the end of their lives.

In these circumstances how can they possibly expect these children to be nice and obedient to them? And if they do expect so, it would be like the parents who want to make their blind children see. Of course, it is not the fault of their children if they disrespect, disobey and misbehave their parents: It is due to the miserable fact that they have been taught by their parents to do so. Such parents are all the more to be pitied. They have no doubt born all the pains and pricks of the cherishment of their children fairly and devotedly but due to their ignorance or carelessness, whatever the case may be, they did not teach their children what they should do and what they should not. Consequently they have to bear whatever treatment their children are giving out to them. They have to reap what they have sown.

According to a Hadis narrated by Hazrat Noman; his father once took him to the Holy Prophet and said, "O' Messenger of Allah! be a witness that I have gifted him some of my (such and such) belongings." The Holy Prophet enquired, "Have you gifted such things to all of your children? Hazrat Noman replied in the negative. The Holy Prophet then said. "In that case make someone else your witness. Do not you like it that all of your children should behave you nicely alike? He replied that he did want that. The Holy Prophet said, "Then do not act like this."

(Al-Adab-Al-Mufrad).

Rights of Children

*The gist of this Hadis lies in the portion. "Do not you like that all of your children should behave you nicely alike? "This connotes the universal truth that the children learn to behave according to the behaviour of their parents. Parents should be extremely careful about their behaviour with the children. If they will not treat them equally, the deprived ones will feel themselves inferior to those who are favoured. Thus disliking the partial behaviour of their parents they will also treat them with indifference on the one hand and they will themselves be psychologically harmed on the other.

Consciousness About The Rights Of Children

Every mother wants her children to be perfect men and women who should come out as ideal and important units of society. This is no doubt a noble and valuable desire, but actually the desires are not fulfilled by mere prayers-unless one practically endeavours to get them fulfilled. In order to make their future bright and to see them successful in their later lives, a mother has to be fully conscious and well informed about the rights of children and fulfil her maternal duties sincerely. This will go a long way in teaching them how to achieve their rights and fulfil their duties. Mothers who are not fully aware of the rights of their children, can never fulfil their maternal duties properly.

Mothers should, all the more, be sincere, and should play active part in giving the children their rights as it is their religious duty as well. According to a saying of the Holy Prophet, "And woman is the caretaker of her husband's house and his children. So you all (in your individual capacities) are the caretakers and you all will be questioned about those who are given in your charge."

Muslim Parents

Though the father is equally responsible for looking after the children, but as he usually remains out for the economic pursuits, the mother remains all the time at house and gets more time and opportunity to live with the children. That is why she is more close to them and they are more free with her than the father. Hence she is considered to be more responsible for training and moulding the characters of children than her husband.

Moreover Almighty Allah has gifted the woman with all the qualities required for the fulfilment of her duties towards the children, much more efficiently than man. Her tendencies and capacity for patience, sacrifice, kindness, benevolence, tenderness and love surpass than those of man. These qualities were required for ideal and balanced cherishment of children.

Importance of Children

The first and most important right of children is that they should be valued and given proper importance by the parents. The parents, instead of getting fed up with the children as an unnecessary burden, should take them as the gifts and bounties from Almighty Allah, otherwise they would remain unable to give them their due rights. Unless they do not realize the worth of their children, they would not be able to accord them sincere love, affection and to take pains and make sacrifices for them.

Islam also gives the children the credit of being the best reward for their parents. They are the best helpers of the parents in carrying out the religious affairs and their best heirs after their death. They are the custodians and upholders of religious beliefs and traditions of their parents. For this very reason the Prophet prayed to Almighty Allah,

> "O' My Lord, grant me from Thyself nice children."
> (3:38)

By this he meant to have those children who would be his religious heirs and carry on the mission of their father. At another place he prayed,

> "O' My Lord, give me an inheritor from You who may be my heir and may also inherit the heritage of the children of Yaqoob." (19: 5-6)

Here he wanted to have children who would keep the flame

of his mission burning which was enkindled by Hazrat Yaqoob and his family. In fact pious children are the best means for their parents to be rewarded here and Hereafter both.

Distinct Castle In Paradise

In case the parents bear the loss of death of their children with patience and thankfulness to Almighty Allah, they will be rewarded well by Him in their lives after death. They will get a castle built in Paradise for them which will be called "The Castle of Gratitude". Hazrat Abu Moosa Ashari quotes the following Hadis in this context:

"When the child of a person dies, Almighty Allah asks His angels 'Have you extracted the soul of my slave'? The angels say 'yes'. Then he again asks, "Have you extracted the soul of the part of his heart (child)! They angels reply "Yes". He then further asks, "Then what My slave said"? The angels reply, "Your slave praised You and recited the following verse on this ordeal.

Inna Lillahe Wa Inna Ilaihe Rajeoon[1]   (2:156)

(We are for Allah and unto Him, We shall return). Hearing this Almighty Allah commands the angels, "Construct a castle in paradise for (this) slave of Mine and name it 'The Castle of Gratitude.' (Jame Tirmizi)

According to another saying of the Holy Prophet narrated by Hazrat Umm-e-Habibah:

"I was sitting with Hazrat 'Aishah when the Holy Prophet

---

1. The Holy Prophet has advised the Muslims to recite the verse on the occasion of death and other calamities so that they should console themselves, on such occasions, by the fact that whatever happens in this world is Willed by Almighty Allah.

Importance of Children

of Almighty Allah came there and said, "If three children of a couple die without reaching the age of adulthood, they will stay at the gate of paradise on the day of Resurrection. When they will be asked to step in, they will reply, we cannot enter the paradise unless our parents accompany us. "Then Allah will tell them, 'Go you and your parents all to paradise.' (Tabrani)

Children — A Continuous Source Of Reward (Sadaqa-i-Jariah)

Children are a continuous source of reward for their parents. If the parents die before their children, they will continuously be rewarded after death on behalf of the virtuous deeds of their children. Leaving behind pious and virtuous children implies an act of virtue which is rewarded even after the death of these parents. It is just like leaving behind big and shady trees under whose shade people take rest and shelter and the credit goes to the person who planted and looked after them. Hazrat Abu Hurairah narrates the following Hadith:

"When a person dies, his period of activity comes to an end except three virtuous deeds due to which he goes on getting the reward from Almighty Allah till eternity. These are:

(1) Leaving behind, some virtuous deed which could continue even after his demise;

(2) The knowledge and information through which people may benefit themselves; and

(3) Virtuous children who should continue praying for him." (Muslim).

Muslim Parents

At another place Hazrat Abu Hurairah says:

'When a deceased person gets upgraded in his life Hereafter he would ask surprisingly as to how it happened after all? He would be told from Almighty Allah that it is due to the perpetual prayers by his children for him, (and Almighty Allah accepted these prayers)."

Killing One's Own Children

The Muslim society is presently suffering from degeneration and decay the world over. So much so that its members have lost the courage to make any progress in their religious or social fields. However despite all these weaknesses, still Muslim parents can and do differentiate between the minor and major digressions from the path of virtues. They cannot even imagine to kill their own child themselves. Islam has played a twofold role in eliminating this cold-blooded crime.

(1) It created the consciousness of respect and importance for human life in the minds of parents and declared killing of children a crime equivalent to shirk (ascribing partners to Almighty Allah).

(2) It is said in the Holy Quran:

("O' My Messenger) Say: Come, I will recite unto you that which your Lord had prohibited for you: that you ascribe nothing as partner to Him and that you do good to parents, and that you slay not your children because of poverty. (6:52)

The Holy Prophet gave so much importance to the eradication of this inhuman and cold-blooded felony that he got

Importance of Children

it included in the Oath of Allegiance made by the Ansar (inhabitants of Medina), who embraced Islam on his hands at Aqabah, that they shall not kill their children. Particularly all the women who came to take the Oath of Allegiance to Islam before him were forbidden to kill their infant children thereafter. Once he came to a gathering of women on the occasion of Eid and forbade them strictly to do so.

Hazrat 'Ubadah-bin-Samit relates that once he and some others were present before the Holy Prophet, who said to them,

> "Promise me that you will never, ascribe partners with Allah, steal, commit any sexual crime, and kill your children. Whoever keeps this promise will get his reward from Allah. One who commits any of these crimes and gets punished by the law, will be atoned. And if his crime is not detected and he is not punished in this world then it is upto Allah to forgive or punish him."
>
> (Bukhari)

Reasons For Killing Children

This cruel tradition was rampant in many countries before the advent of Islam. Romans and Indian Rajputs frequently and openly killed their children. The pagan Arabs excelled all others in this inhuman practice.

Usually children were killed by the parents for three reasons:

(1) Some illiterate and Superstitious tribes did this as a ritual in order to please their gods and goddesses. They used to sacrifice their children so that their gods might be appeased and give them rain, victory in war, health etc. Or they vowed before their gods to sacrifice their children at their

Muslim Parents

altars if their wish was fulfilled. Most surprisingly the women were also a party to the execution of this crime.

Once a woman came to Hazrat Abdullah-bin-Abbas and said that she had vowed to sacrifice her child. He forbade her to do so and asked her to give proper compensation for her vow.

(Mo'atta Imam Malik)

This heinous practice is not a memory of the past. Most surprisingly, even in this twentieth century, people perform this ritual to prove that there are still such superstitious and heartless parents who take the life of their own flesh and blood by their own hands. The following news appeared in Daily Dawat, New Delhi, India on April 18, 1975:

"A nine year old girl was sacrificed at the alter of goddess Lakshmi (goddess of wealth in Hindu religion) in a village of Warangal District, on March 24; The Police have arrested a farmer and his 21 year old daughter on the charges of murder and have recovered from their possession the silver bracelets and gold earrings of the deceased."

The Holy Quran also indicates towards such persons and declared that they are but the losers.

> "Thus have their (so called partners of Allah) made the killing of their children to seem fair to many of the idolaters that they may ruin them and make their faith obscure for them." (6:138)

And at another place it is said:

> "They are the losers who besottedly have slain their children without knowledge." (6:141)

Importance of Children

(2) People killed their children due to the fear that they will add to their financial worries and make their lives more miserable. Such parents thought their children as an unnecessary burden upon their shoulders as they would have been fed, clothed and looked after by them. But they did not know, until the Last Messenger of Allah told them that they should not worry about that. He told them, that it was Almighty Allah not they, Who provided the sustenance for them and their children. He is the only Sustainer of all. When He sends a new person in this world He also creates means for his sustenance.

According to the Holy Quran:

> 'Kill not your children for fear of poverty. It is We who provide for them and for you. Surely the killing of them is a great sin. (17:13)

Hazrat Abdullah bin Mas'ood narrates that once he asked the Holy Prophet to tell him the greatest sin in the eyes of Allah. He replied, "That you ascribe partners with Allah though Only He has created you." Hazrat Abdullah realised to the severity of this sin. He then asked about the next greatest sin, the Holy Prophet replied, "That you kill your child fearing his share in your livelihood." When further asked, he replied "That you commit adultery with the wife of your neighbour."

(3) Another reason for this murderous tradition is most idiotic and its mode is most inhuman and most brutal. Particularly in the pre-Islamic Arabia some people used to bury their newborn daughters alive for the sake of their false pride.

They thought it extremely humiliating and insulting to have a son-in-law who would possess their daughters as wives. The very thought of the existence of a daughter was repulsive to them. They felt very much indignated in marrying their daughters to others while thinking as they totally forgot the fact, that they themselves have the daughters of others as their wives. They were the victims of their false notions of pride and dignity. So whenever they knew that a female child was born to them they immediately tried to get rid of her, usually by burying her alive. The Holy Quran describes it in these words.

> "When if one of them receives tidings of the birth of female, his face remains darkened, and he is worth inwardly. He hides himself from the folk because of the evil of that of which he has had tidings, (asking himself); Shall he keep it in contempt, or bury it beneath the dust. Verily evil is their judgment." (16:58, 59)

As described earlier the tradition of burying the new born female children alive was very much in vogue in some Arab tribes. They took pride in doing so and used to mention their "dare deeds" with exaltation. One of such maniacs came to the Holy Prophet boasting that he had buried her eight daughters alive with her own hands.

The Ordeal of the Innocent Girl

The people of the tribe of Banu Tameem in Pre-Islamic Arabia were most prone towards this inhuman practice. The Chief of this tribe Qais bin Asim, after embracing Islam confessed to the Holy Prophet in the following words:

"O' Messenger of Allah! a daughter was born to me when I was away from home on a journey: Taking advantage of my absence her mother, out of natural urge, nursed her for few days. After some days fearing that I might not bury her alive,

Importance of Children

she sent the child to her sister to be cherished by her. She thought that I would be merciful to the child when she would become of some age and would not harm her. When I came back home from the journey I was told that my wife had given birth to a dead child. Thus the matter was shelved. The child remained being cherished by her aunt for some years. Once I went out of the house for the whole day. Thinking that I was out for a long time my wife considered it quite safe to call her daughter and enjoy her company for sometime in my absence.

Quite unexpectedly, I changed my mind and came back home earlier. When I entered the home I saw a very beautiful and a tidy little girl playing in the house. When I looked at her I suddenly felt a surge of strong and spontaneous love for her within me. My wife also sensed it and became sure that blood had called blood and my fatherly love and affection has sprung up for the child. I asked her "O my good wife! whose child is it? How charming she is!"

Then my wife told me all about her. I could not control myself and eagerly took her in my arms. Her mother told her that I was her father and she began loving me dearly calling me "O' my father, O' my father," every now and then. At those moments I felt an indescribable pleasure by embracing her while she put her arms around my neck.

Days went by in this way and the child remained being nourished by us free from any worry or discomfort. But at times when she caught my attention such thoughts came to my mind; I shall have to be a father-in-law by giving her off to someone in marriage. I shall have to bear the insult that my daughter will be someone's wife. How shall I be able to face people? All my honour and pride will be ruined. These thoughts took hold of my mind and tortured me incessantly. At last these thoughts roused my indignation and made me devoid of any more patience at all. Then I decided to do away with this stigma of shame and humiliation for me and my ancestors. I decided to bury the girl alive.

I asked my wife to make the girl ready as I would take her to a feast with me. My wife gave her a bath, clad her in pretty clothes and made her ready to go with me. The little girl was also bubbling with cheerfulness, thinking that she was accompanying her father on a happy occasion. I started with her towards a jungle. The child was going with me leaping with joy and pleasure, holding my hand here, getting ahead of me there, prattling to me with queaks of innocent gaiety and laughter. But I had become blind to see and enjoy these innocent acts and was impatient to get rid of her as soon as possible. The poor child was absolutely unaware of my sinister intention and followed me merrily.

At last I stopped to a lonely spot and started digging the ground. The innocent child was surprised to see me doing that and repeatedly asked, Father, why you are digging the earth? But I did not pay any heed to her queries. How could she possibly know that I was digging that pit to bury my own cheerful and beautiful daughter in it with my own hands?

While digging the earth the dust would fall upon my feet and clothes. My daughter would clean the dust from my feet and clothes saying, "Father, you are spoiling your clothes." But I like a deaf person did not even care to look at her as if I had not heard her at all. I continued my vicious job and dug a pit enough to serve my purpose. Then I suddenly threw the innocent child into the pit and hastily began filling it. The poor child was

Importance of Children

looking at me with frightened and surprised eyes. She was frantically crying and screaming, "Father, my dear father what is this? "What are you doing? I have done nothing at all. Father please why are you hiding me in the ground? But I kept on doing my work like a deaf, dumb and blind person without paying the least attention to her beseeching and entreaties. O' Messenger of Allah, I was too cruel and too sadistic and too heartless to have pity on her. On the contrary, after burying my daughter alive I heaved a sigh of relief and came back satisfied that I have saved my honour and pride from humiliation".

Hearing this pathetic and heart-rending incident about the helpless, innocent child the Holy Prophet could not control himself and tears started falling down upon his cheeks. While the tears rolled down from his eyes he said, "This is extreme cruelty. How one, who does not pity others, can be pitied by Almighty Allah?"

The Woeful True Story

Once a person told the Holy Prophet his own story of the days of ignorance. The story was so pathetic that it made the Messenger of Allah very gloomy. He related:

"O' Messenger of Allah, we are illiterate and we had no knowledge and no guidance. We worshipped the idols and killed our children with our own hands. O' Messenger of Allah, I had a little and a very charming daughter. Whenever I would call her she would run into my arms laughing with joy and pleasure. She was quite free with me. One day I called her to me. She readily came to me as usual. I asked her to follow me. I was going a bit ahead of her and she was running after me with her small and infirm steps. There was a deep well at a short distance from my house. When I reached at the well I stopped and the child also came there trotting behind me. O' Messenger of Allah I caught hold of the child by the hand and threw her into the well. The poor child kept on crying and calling me from inside the well. "Father O' my dear father."O' Messenger of Allah! these were her last words.

When the man finished the heart piercing story tears were rolling down from the eyes of the Holy Prophet out of sheer grief and pity for the innocent child. One of the companions of the Holy Prophet who was present on this occasion reprimanded the person that he made the Holy Prophet sad by telling him the woeful story. To this the Prophet of Allah replied, "Do not scold him, do not admonish him. He has come to me for the redressal of his sin." Then addressing the person he asked him to repeat the painful story. The person retold the incident. While the person was repeating his touching story the Holy Prophet was so deeply moved that his beard wetted with tears. When the person finished repeating the unhappy incident the Holy Prophet told him:

"By the virtue of embracing Islam all the sins committed by you during pre-Islamic life are forgiven (by Almighty Allah). Go now and be virtuous." (Musnad Darimi).

Only Almighty Allah knows how many innocent and helpless girls became the victim of this cruel and heinous crime and for how long daughters were being buried alive by their own fathers during the dark period of ignorance in the Arabian society. Though even in those days there were some sensible and kind hearted persons who did try their best to save the innocent little girls from the cruel and inhuman practice. But these individuals and solitary efforts could not eradicate this atrocious custom from the society.

Importance of Children

Eradication of the Evil of Burying the Daughters Alive

Farzdoq was a famous poet of Arabia. He was very much proud of his paternal grandfather Hazrat S'asah who saved many girls from being buried alive in a period when Arabs felt humiliated even by imagining themselves to be the father of a girl. Hazrat S'asah narrates his own story in the following words:

"Once I went in search of my two camels which were lost. In my way I spotted a kindling fire at a distance. I thought that I should go there. It came my mind that the fire might have been enkindled by someone who needs help. I started to walk towards the fire with the decision to help the person if he requires. I made my camel to trot faster and soon I reached at the place where the fire was burning. It was in the precincts of the tribe of Banu Anmar. When I reached there I saw an old man with shaggy hairs sitting in front of his house in a pensive mood. Heart piercing cries of a woman were coming from inside the house. After the exchange of compliments with the old man I asked him as to what was happening there. He told me that his wife was under-going birth pangs for the last three days. During the conversation someone said loudly from inside the house that the child was born. Immediately the old man cried, "It is alright if it is a boy, but I do not want to hear even its voice if it is a girl. I will kill her instantly. I cannot afford to have a girl. And by the Will of Almighty it was a girl."

I implored to the old man meekly, "O' Shaikh, please, do not kill her, after all it is your own child. As far as her sustenance is concerned you should not worry at all as Almighty Allah is the only Sustainer." The old man did not pay any attention to what I said and again roared with anger, "No, never, I cannot leave her alive. I will not rest till I kill her." I again beseeched him to spare the life of the innocent infant in a very humble tone. He frowned at me and retorted back, "If your heart is bleeding so much for the child why do not you buy her and cherish her yourself." I readily agreed to the proposal and paying the demanded price of the infant brought her to my house in very high spirits. I promised to Almighty Allah that I will bring up this child with love and kindness. I also promised to Almighty Allah that whenever some heartless person will intend to kill an innocent girl, I will not let him do so. Instead I will pay the ransom to the cruel and get her free to come with me. I will keep her with me and cherish her with utmost love and affection. So I kept on fulfilling my promise till Almighty Allah made Hazrat Mohammed (S.A.W.) His Prophet. By that time I had saved ninety four of girls from being killed by their cruel fathers. Afterwards the Holy Prophet, through his impressive preachings and strict forbiddings, got this inhuman tradition eradicated from the Muslim Society, the world over."   (Al-Aghani).

Islam enjoys the biggest credit of purging the Muslim Society from the curse of killing the children in all its, forms. Our sacred religion made it one of the marks of identification of Muslims, near and dear to Almighty Allah that they go on praying to Him to make their children most beloved to them. The Holy Quran says:

> "And those who says: Our Lord, vouchsafe us comfort of our wives and of our offsprings, and make us patterns for (all) those who ward off (evil)."   (25-74)

Birth of a Girl

Birth of a child brings happiness to us. Naturally we should feel like that and also expect our relatives, friends and neighbours

Importance of Children

to share our happiness and joy in this matter, and it usually happens like that. For according to the commandments of Almighty Allah and in the light of the very behaviour of our Holy Prophet, we cannot even imagine to differentiate between a male and a female child and treat them differently. To be happy over the birth of a boy and becoming sad in case of the birth of a girl, to repel the very existence of a daughter and being elated to have a son, to give preference to the sons over the daughters, these all are un-Islamic and unhealthy attitudes and a blot upon Muslim Society.

Nevertheless, there are many Muslim families where completely different treatment is meted out to the male and female children by their parents. They take the birth of a girl as a misfortune. Elderly persons, on such occasions are seen consoling the gloomy parents, particularly the fathers that "daughters are a boon from Almighty Allah, they are more loving to their parents than the sons, they do not give you any trouble, they serve you better", and so on and so forth. The parents listen to all these consolations but with a heavy heart. Outwardly they show their agreement with the congratulators and sympathizers but they are so grieved from within as some calamity has befallen them, thinking how happy they would have been had a son would have been born to them instead of a daughter.

On the contrary if they are bestowed with a son their joy, elation and happiness knows no bounds. The mother, after giving birth to a son, looks at the all smiling father with a look of pride and exaltation in her eyes. An inner sense of pride, satisfaction and gratitude surge through the hearts of both. Now they would be able to hold their heads high and would inform the people

Muslim Parents

with pride and exaltation that a son has been born to them. On the other hand relatives, friends, acquaintances all would congratulate them heartily. The auspicious occasion will be celebrated with different sorts of merriment and pleasure extravagantly

But we should never forget even for a single moment that the birth of a man or a female child is beyond our control. We do not have any say at all in this matter. It is not the matter of our will but the will of Almighty Allah who Himself controls the issue. Only He knows well who deserves a son and to whom suits a daughter. We can only wish and pray to have a male or a female child. But the decision rests with Almighty Allah who is the creator of all males and females at His own sweet will. Only He may give us a boy or a girl or even none at all regardless of our wishes and desires. There is none who could make Him change His decision by whatever wishes or entreaties one makes. He is the only One who does whatever He likes. According to the Holy Quran:

> "To Allah belongs the sovereignty of the heavens and the earth. He creates what He wills. He bestows female (offspring) upon whom He wills, and bestows male (offspring) upon whom He wills. Or He mingles them, males and females and He makes barren whom He wills. He is knower, powerful. (42:49, 50)

Actually the human beings are totally helpless in this regard. Even the modern science and technology which have enabled man to temporarily inhabit to Moon, to prevent disastrous epidemics and to produce Atom, Hydrogen, Cobalt and Neutron bombs have not yet solved the mystery of birth and the determination of the sex of the embryo. Any physician, spiritualist

Importance of Children

or exorcist on earth can neither foretell the sex of an unborn child nor can make any barren women capable of pregnancy. It is totally beyond their means. It is a painful fact that many a Muslim women fall pray to bogus and professional spiritualists and quacks in the hope that these cheats will "bless" them with particularly the male children or enable them to get pregnant through their foolish rituals, charms and harmful notions. This is a mere superstition and fanaticism.

Moreover, we cannot know whether we would be benefitted and comforted by the male or the female children. It is often seen that a family in which there are many daughters but no son is full of peace, satisfaction and other bounties from Almighty Allah. On the contrary there are several homes which consist of several sons but no daughters. And these sons have come out to be the source of constant worry, anxiety and even humiliation for their parents. In several cases it is found that, after giving birth of several sons a mother earnestly prayed to Almighty Allah to give her a daughter. But when prayers were granted and she got a daugther, that besought girl proved to be a constant menace and a stigma of shame and indignation for her poor parents. And the poor mother who so earnestly longed for her birth became compelled to cry in remorse, "I wish you were dead just when you were born." Still there are homes where the sons break the heart of their parents while the daughters are the boons to the parents who are short of words to express their love, service and obedience to them. So only Allah knows whether we deserve sons or daughters or none of them at all.

The Blessed Daughter

The wife of Imran vowed that if a son was born to her, she would bequeath him to Almighty Allah. She prayed to the Creator

Muslim Parents

to accept her humble offer. But He so willed that she gave birth to a daughter. She was extremely pained and gloomy. Broken hearted she moaned, "O' Almighty Allah: I got a daughter in place of a son. How shall she serve the purpose for which I needed a son and made my vow. A female is very much different than a male. She, due to some biological handicaps, unlike men, shall not be able to serve and worship you vigorously consistently. O' my Sustainer! what shall I do now?" But she did not know that her wailings and remorse were baseless. She was totally unaware of the fact that the very girl will prove to be the source of reward, recompense and exaltation for her. That due to the girl her name will be mentioned in the holy scriptures and crores of people will read it till the end of this world. And that she will have the honour of becoming the maternal grandmother of the pious Messenger to whom Almighty Allah will reveal the Holy Bible (Injeel): So Almighty Allah did not, as she thought, discard the wish of the wife of Imran. Instead He accepted her prayer beyond her desires and made this acceptance glorious, sacred and immortal by mentioning it in the Holy Quran in the following words:—

> "And her Allah accepted her with full acceptance and vouchsafed to her a goodly growth; and made Zachariah her guardian. Whenever Zachariah went into the sanctuary where she was, he found that she had food. He said: O Mariam from where comes to you this (food)? She answered; It is from Allah. Allah gives without stint to whom He wills." (7:37)

Children are the gifts from Almighty Allah whether it is a son or a daughter, both are alike and do not make any difference at all. It is the duty of a Muslim who receives any of these gifts

Importance of Children

to be highly grateful to Him who has been beneficent enough to bestow him the gift. It is quite unbefitting for a true Believer to be ungrateful to Almighty Allah on whatever He bestows to him. Only He knows best what we should get from Him. He decides according to His own sweet Will and most judicious Judgements which are unique and final. As the slaves of Almighty Allah, we have to accept these Judgements with submission and gratitude. It is our foremost duty to firmly believe that whatever He gives us or takes from us is in our best interests and we have to be content with it. This should be the attitude of all true Muslims.

Each and every Muslim undoubtedly believes that none has so far been born, nor any one will be, having a status higher than our Holy Prophet Hazrat Muhammad (P.B.U.H.). He had four daughters from his beloved wife Hazrat Khadeejah. Once he told about her that she was the best of all women on earth or in Heaven. Another Hadith runs:

> "Do not hate your daughters. I am also the father of (several) daughters."

According to another one:

> "Daughters are very loving and they are potent source of affluence and welfare (for the parents)".
>
> (Knaz-al-Ummad)

Hazrat Ibn-i-Sareet narrates that once he heard the Holy Prophet saying:

> "When a female child is born Almighty Allah sends His angels to that house. They come to the dwellers of that house and pray that may peace be upon them. The angel then cover the new born girl under the shadow of their

wings and caressing the head of the baby with their hands say that his is a weak and frail person who is given birth by a weak and frail person. Whoever will bear the responsibility of her cherishment will go on having the blessings of Almighty Allah as long as that person remains alive." (Al Mojam al Saghir li Tabarani)

Once a man was sitting with Hazrat Abdullah bin Umar. He had several daughters: He said in anguish, "I wish all my daughters are dead," Hazrat Abdullah became angry to hear that and he rebuffed the man with the reproaching querry, "Are you their sustainer?"

It is the most beneficent favour from Almighty Allah that he has honoured us by giving us daughters. He has given us the tidings of Heaven for having daughters. It means that He wants us to value the daughters like sons. We should cherish them without any differentiation and give them the same amount of love, kindness, affection and importance which we give to our sons. Rather we should be more kind and nice in our behaviour with the daughters as they live with us temporarily. They put up with us upto a certain period and then go to their husbands to make their own homes. Who knows what sort of treatment they get from the persons with whom they are related after marriage. We should give them the chance to remember our nice and kind treatment to console themselves in their moments of grief and sorrow if they are not behaved well by their husbands or other members of his family.

For these and many other potent reasons the Messenger of Almighty Allah has mentioned daughters as a "shield" from the fire of Hell and "means" for the entry into the Heaven.

Sustenance of Children

The second right of the children is to be nourished and brought up by the parents. After their birth the children have also to depend upon the parents for their cherishment. Infants are helpless to a certain period of life during which they need constant help and care for their survival and growth. It is only the parents who are capable of providing care and protection to them in the most befitting manner. If the children are deprived of this treatment by the parents they cannot survive. If they are given this help in an improper insufficient way by the parents they are sure to get unbalanced and immature personalities. In view of this Islam has made it the next important duty of the parents to cherish their children in a proper and befitting manner.

Natural Love for Children

Sustenance of children is a very difficult and painstaking job. Extreme degree of love, affection, patience, sacrifice and consideration are required to bring them up. Almighty Allah, by His Grace, has created immense love and affection in the hearts of parents for their children. This love enables the parents to nourish their children so lovingly that none can be paralleled to them. They take all the pains and undergo all the hardships and difficulties with pleasure in cherishing them. Instead of getting impatient and fed up with their offsprings they feel satisfied rather elated and exalted by serving them so labouriously and painfully. They forget all these pains and pricks when they cast a glance at there growing children and a deep surge of satisfaction and pride fills their hearts. In fact Almighty Allah has done a great favour to us by creating in us the feelings of extreme and abundant love and attachment with our children. Had it been otherwise, the parents would have found it a terrible ordeal to fulfil their onerous duty of cherishing the children in a proper way.

Almighty Allah has created the feelings of love and affection in the hearts of all parents irrespective of their religion, beliefs even if they are atheists. He made it natural for the parents to love their children and cherish them so that they may survive and do the same in their turn for the healthy propagation of this world. Naturally everyone wishes to see his children achieve a status higher than his own in the world and also inherit the wealth, property and the values, customs and traditions of his culture. When those who, due to their backwardness and illiteracy, do not have the consciousness of their responsibilities towards their children have the same natural feelings of love and affection for their children. To nurse and care the child, the mother is the ideal person. Even in animals this sentiment of maternal love and affection for their offsprings, though in a lesser degree, is found without any exception. Almighty Allah has so willed that each and every species must have these feelings so that they may grow and survive.

A Muslim Mother

A mother who is devoid of Islam has a limited approach to life. She only thinks about the worldly life the life on earth, but she does not have any conception of the life hereafter. She has all the feelings of love and affection for her children as it is a natural phenomenon. She cherishes the children with the hope

Sustenance of Children

that by doing so her race would be preserved, that the children, after coming an age, would care for them in their old age, and they may be fully prepared and equipped for their future life.

But the Muslim mother, in addition to all these hopes and expectations, cherishes her children with the firm belief that her attitude towards the offsprings will definitely reflect upon her life in hereafter in which she has a staunch faith. Her mode of thinking is altogether different. She cherishes her children also with the view that if she nurtured them according to the instructions given by Islam, she would be richly rewarded by Almighty Allah in her eternal life. She thinks that in doing so she will have the pleasure of Almighty Allah who will pardon her sins and award her the Heaven for fulfilling this sacred duty ascribed to her by Him. She fears that if she did not bring up her children according to His commandments and the teachings of His holy Prophet she would surely earn His wrath and liable to be put into Hell.

She, no doubt, cherishes her children due to the natural urge to do so. She also does with a thought to be benefited during her worldly life where she would need the love and affection from them in her hour of need. But the most potent factor which makes her most conscious and duty bound in this regard is her desire to be benefited and rewarded in her another life which is eternal and where she will badly need the pleasure of Almighty Allah to live a comfortable and luxurious life.

This mode of thinking and action is very much beneficial in conditions where the children, even after the hectic efforts of parents and their valuable sacrifices for them, still become wayward, headstrong, disobedient and short of their expectations.

Then these Muslim parents will not be disappointed, frustrated and remorseful due to the belief that what they did not get from their children they will get it from Almighty Allah in both the lives particularly in the life to come. They know well that they have fulfilled their duty as He commanded them and He never overlooks the virtuous deeds of His slaves and rewards them in a befitting manner. This belief will console them and keep them calm and satisfied, as the rewards from Almighty Allah surpass all the rewards of the world. According to the Holy Quran:

> "(And it will be said to them) This is a reward for you. Your endeavours (upon earth) have found acceptance (of Allah)." (76:22)

Almighty Allah is so bountiful upon His obedient slaves that He encourages them and increases their capacity to perform virtuous deeds and rewards them many times more than their deeds. Moreover He overlooks minor mistakes and only takes into account the virtue underlying the act done by them for earning His pleasure. He says in the Holy Quran:

> "And whosoever earns good we increase that good for him. Verily Allah is oft-Forgiving, the Appreciator (of good)." (42:33)

The Responsibilities in Nourishing the Children

Nourishment of children is the responsibility of mother and father both and they fulfil it with each other's cooperation. Actually cherishment of children involves two great responsibilities.

Sustenance of Children

(1) To nurse and bring up the children.
(2) To spend upon the cherishment of the children.

The first responsibility consists of nursing, feeding and protection so that they may survive and grow properly to become responsible persons during their later lives. While the Second one requires the parents to bear all the expenses of their children, till their adulthood, regarding food, clothes, health, education and other related fields.

Division of these responsibilities

The first responsibility, though seemingly to be shared together, is mostly shouldered by the mother. Islam has all the more made it maternal by making it her duty to feed the child from her breasts for at least two years.

The second one is particularly the responsibility of the father. He is to take care of the financial and economic needs of the children while the mother is left to attend to other duties.

The Real Sphere of Womens' Activities

Islam has specially allocated to the women the domestic work. She plays the most important role, remaining inside the home most of the time, is cherishing the children and moulding their personalities. This is her true field of activity and by her behaviour in this field she is judged as successful or otherwise. This is her real job for which she will be enquired on the Day of Judgment. According to a saying of the Holy Prophet:

> "The woman (wife) is the caretaker of and responsible for the house of her husband. She would be held accountable for the persons and things given in her charge." (Agreed Upon)

Muslim Parents

It is a known fact that whenever and wherever woman was lured to neglect her domestic life by the glitter and glamour of the outside world and she indulged in economic and other unbecoming pursuits her home was ruined. Her own as well as the lives of her children were wrecked and they lost their peace of mind. In most of these cases their peaceful home atmosphere was torn to pieces and their children became wayward and delinquents. In the developing countries where the women have not yet fully realized the hazards of the so called "Womens' Liberation," and emancipation of women movements, they are coming out of their homes and indulging in the economic and professional pursuits to prove that they are not at all inferior to men in any field. They are trying to prove themselves to be free and equal to men by even going beyond their means. They are now trying to earn to show that they are no longer dependent upon men for their sustenance. This economic freedom, they think, will alleviate their subordination to men and will establish their equality with men.

But the countries in which women have been given the so called rights of freedom and equality and left free to do as they wish are now shedding the tears of remorse over the pathetic plight of their degenerating and disintegrating societies. Their women being economically and socially independent, are no longer faithful and dedicated daughters, wives, sisters and mothers. Marriage has become an outdated and old fashioned custom. Instead they prefer, companionship, which involves no binding on the part of the man or woman. Children of such parents usually become young delinquents and drug addicts. The whole society is decaying and disintegrating fast. They have reached at a point of no return. The world renowned western scholar and thinker Arnold Toynbee laments,

Sustenance of Children

"In human history the periods which have been plagued with decay and degeneration are those in which women have stepped outside their homes".

Dr.Joad writes, "I have firm belief that this world will transform into Heaven if women should be content in cherishing their children and fulfilling their domestic responsibilities." (As quoted by "Asia"April 25, 1956 Lahore).

Our Holy Prophet had warned his ummah (followers) much earlier that the worst period for the Muslims will be when they would be dominated by their women who would be the sole managers of their collective affairs.

He further said:

"When your rulers and caretakers are wicked and your affluents are misers and your affairs are looked after by the women then your death is better than your life."
(Mishkat)

He told the Muslim Women that if they performed their natural and social duties they would dwell with him in Heaven. It obviously means that the zenith of the success of women is the proper fulfilment of their natural and domestic duties which are highly appreciated by Almighty Allah. The Holy Prophet said:

"The woman who remained within her home to take care of her children will be with me in Paradise."
(Kanz-ul-Ummal)

What other tidings a Muslim woman would cherish than of

being with the Holy Messenger of Allah in Heaven? And this honour can be achieved by any woman who prefers to look after her children and other members of the family, which is her true obligation, rather than neglecting it for the sake of other pursuits outside her home.

Actually the creator has given the specific attributes to the females - their physical structure, their special finer, soft and tender feelings, their religious, ethical and moral attitude and their whole temperament for the very purpose of making their homes a replica of paradise where all are happy and satisfied. It will be an injustice to let them leave their natural place and perform the duties which are against their nature and for which they have not been created.

Almighty Allah has put in the nature of women great flexibility and tenderness. He has bestowed them the extreme degree of patience and forbearance, selflessness and sacrifice, service and sincerety, care and compassion, kindness and devotion and love and affection together with the natural urge to love and cherish their children. Consequently she bears the most onerous and most important responsibility of bringing up her children. In fulfilling this nerve-wrecking duty she feels pleased and satisfied instead of showing any signs of displeasure or perturbance.

On the contrary men have not been given these qualities with such abundance and intensity as the females. They are, by nature, are meant for shouldering the responsibility of nursing and cherishing the children in this manner. They are neither suited nor have the time to fulfil this duty. Almighty Allah has allocated him the responsibility of earning to cater for the economic and other needs of his dependents. Both have been awarded separate qualities and capabilities in accordance with their separate fields of activity. Thus Almighty Allah has struck a pleasant balance and equilibrium in the collective life of the couple so that they smoothly manage and run their conjugal life and fulfil their domestic responsibilities through mutual cooperation.

The Best Role of Women

To think the domestic life and cherishment of children insulting and below their dignity while taking pride in carrying out outdoor and collective activities are wrong and unhealthy notions. Though Islam has no doubt given to the women the permission to a certain extent, to participate in the matters other than domestic ones, but it never means that they should cross the limits and take undue advantage of this permission. They should not be so lured towards the outside world so as to neglect and grudge their domestic duties in order to prove themselves advanced and progressive. The progress and development of human culture and civilization implies the establishment of an ideal and peaceful society. But such a society can never be established unless the children of a nation are fully prepared and well equipped during their early stages of life, to be the best citizens in their later lives. Only this will ensure the creation of a model society. And this can only be done by the mothers. Auguste Comte, the well-known sociologist who enjoys the honour to be the father of sociology stressed the importance of the role of women in the establishment of a sound and balanced society by moulding the personalities of their offsprings appropriately.

(Scientific struggle for Social Reconstruction).

Muslim Parents

It is now proved that only mothers can accomplish this task in a most befitting manner. The lap of mother is the place where a child gets the basic impressions inculcated upon his mind which go on becoming deeper and deeper throughout his whole life. Good maternal nature produces good children. Due to this potent reason Islam has made it the best role of women. In Islam this role is defined as equivalent to Jihad (the Holy War) and the Holy Prophet has described Jihad as the "Highest peak of religion." He once told Hazrat Muaz:

> "Should I tell you the base, the pillar and the highest peak of religion (Islam)? I replied, 'Please do, O'Messenger of Allah. He then said, "The base of religion is submission, its pillar is salat (Prayer) and its, highest peak is Jihad." (Tirmizi)

In the light of this Hadith the women who are busy in doing their household duties and bringing up the children are doing Jihad and will be rewarded as such. Hazrat Aishah, the beloved wife of the Holy Prophet quotes him:

> "Taking care of your homes is your responsibility. This act of yours is Jihad." (Musnad Ahmad)

At another place he said:

> "The endeavours of a woman to serve and maintain her home would be equal to the act of the Holy warriors (Mujahideen) if Allah so wills." (Kanz-ul-Ummal)

The Holy Prophet further said:

> "A woman right from the period of pregnancy till childbirth and from the birth of the child till the period of lactation

Sustenance of Children

is like that Holy warrior (Mujahid) who is continuously vigilant during his duty. And if she dies during these periods she gets the status of a martyr."

(Kanz-ul-Ummal)

WIDOWED MOTHERS

If the husband of a woman dies early, Islam not only permits her to re-marry but approves the act also. But the woman who, after the untimely death of her husband, does not marry again for the fear that her children may not be treated well by her second husband and dedicates her youthful days to the care and cherishment of children, is a symbol of self control and sacrifices. Islam gives a very high status and appreciates this act of sacrifice of such pious and dutiful women. They are given the tidings of having the company of the Holy Prophet on the day of Judgment. Once the Messenger of Allah said:

> "On the doomsday myself and the woman whose cheeks have been burnt (with grief and worry) will be with each other like the first two fingers of a hand. She was a beautiful girl, coming from a decent family and was deprived of her husband, but she did not remarry for the sake of bringing up her orphan children (in a befitting manner) till her children became self-sufficient or died."
> (Abu Dawood)

A woman can be deprived of her husband due to the death, divorce or separation, whatever the case may be. In Arabic the word "Ayyam" is used for the person who is deprived of a male or female. But here the Holy Prophet used it for a widow particularly. But even if a woman, deprived of her husband through divorce and having the responsibility of looking after the children, does not marry again for the sake of her children, she is also expected to get the same reward by Almighty Allah.

Maternal Role of the Companions of the Holy Prophet

The female companions of the Holy Prophet who believed in his prophethood, eagerly followed his instructions, because they had a firm belief that they would earn the pleasure of Almighty Allah by obeying His Messenger. These pious ladies made exemplary efforts in cherishing their children also. They sacrificed their comforts, longings, and youth for the sake of their children. Actually they had fully absorbed the teachings and instructions of Holy Prophet Muhammad (P.B.U.H.) and applied them in their practical lives.

The Ideal Mother

> "O Almighty Allah! bless my mother. She had no equal in cherishing and looking after me."

These were the words of Hazrat Anas, a faithful servant of the Holy Prophet, about his mother. Her real name was Rumaisah or Sehla, but she was usually known as Umme Saleem. She was the daughter of Milhan who belonged to the Ansars' tribe of Najjar.

She was married to a young man named Malik-bin Nazar who belonged to the same tribe. Hazrat Anas was still a child when she embraced Islam against the will of her husband. Whenever she would make the little child learn the Kalimah he would get much annoyed. He became so disgusted with the Islamic environment in his house that he went to Syria leaving

Sustenance of Children

behind his wife and the little child all alone. While he was in Syria some of his enemies killed him. Now the young lady became widow. Several men sent her the proposals for re-marriage, but she turned down every proposal saying,

> "I will not marry again till my son is grown up and capable of moving in the company of adults. Then I will marry with the consent of Anas."
>
> (Tabaqat Ibn-e-S'ad)

Though she was young and free to marry the man of her choice, but she did not do so as her second husband may not maltreat her little son.

When Hazrat Anas came to be an adult Abu-Talha sent her the proposal to marry him. But how could she marry a non-believer? So she replied him in these wise and effective words:

> "Abu Talha, do not you know that your god whom you are worshipping has grown from the earth? He replied, 'yes I know'. Then are you not ashamed of worshipping a tree?"

Abu Talha was very much impressed by these words. He came back to her after a few days and embraced Islam. She then became satisfied and without giving the least importance to his poverty she accepted his proposal. She told him not to worry about the arrangement of Mehr (Dowry). She said that she did not need any other thing from him after he had embraced Islam as that was her best Mehr. Moreover her marriage took place under the supervision of her beloved son for whose sake she avoided to re-marry for such a long period. Hazrat Anas, on this occasion surprisingly said, "What a strange Mehr of my mother is." The status and esteem gained by this pious woman can be estimated by the following saying of the Holy Prophet. He said:

> "When I entered the paradise I heard the movement of someone. I asked whose footsteps were those? I was told that was Rumaisa, the daughter of Milhan."
> (Sahih Muslim & Tabaqat Ibn-e-S'ad).

Exemplary Sacrifice of Umm-i-Hani

The female follower of the Holy Prophet of his time loved and respected him beyond limitations. But when he sent the proposal of marriage of Umm-i-Hani, the widowed daughter of his beloved uncle Abu-Talib, she declined. Her reply to the Holy Prophet was his appreciation instead of causing any offence. She told the pious Prophet,

> "O Messenger of Almighty Allah! you are dear to me more than my two eyes. But the duties of a wife are huge and onerous. I fear that after marriage I will not be able to provide proper care to my children. And if I remained preoccupied in their care and cherishment I may not have the opportunity of serving my husband as I should." (Tabaqat Ibn-e-S'ad)

She is the same fortunate and pious lady who had the honour of playing hostess to the Holy Prophet. The Holy Messenger of Almighty Allah, on the day of the victory of Mecca, took a bath and offered chasht (after sunrise) prayer in her house. On that day he also forgave the two non-believers whom she had given shelter in her house. (Musnad Ahmad, Vol. 6)

Suckling The Children And Islam

Cherishing the child also implies that mothers should suckle their children, if possible, for the prescribed period. This is the right of a child as well as the natural urge of a mother. It is also an age old tradition of a society that mothers should feed the baby with her milk. To shoulder the responsibilities of pregnancy giving birth and suckling the child for his survival are the natural responsibilities of a mother. And instead of taking these jobs grudgingly she feels pleasure and exaltation in performing them, because she takes them as the rights of her child as well as the duties of her own. According to the Holy Quran:

> "And mothers should suckle for two complete years their children whose fathers so desire to complete the suckling." (2:233)

This verse is particularly meant for those women who have been separated from their husbands through divorce. To be suckled by mother is the natural right of a child while to suckle the child is the religious duty of the mother. This is proved by the instructions contained in the above quoted verse from the Holy Quran for wives who have been divorced or have themselves asked for divorce from their husbands. But it does not mean that this command of Almighty Allah is limited to the above mentioned mothers only. It is quite unimaginable and beyond even simple reason that the mothers who are not divorced may be excluded from the jurisdiction of this command. Both are mothers and cannot be differentiated regarding their maternal duties from each other. The point in particularising this verse for the separated mothers is that they might not deprive their infants of this basic and important right due to the feelings of grudge and abhorance for their husbands. Almighty Allah did not separately command the mothers living with their husbands to suckle their children because there was no need of it at all. For He has made it natural for mothers to suckle their children. Indescribable sensations of love, pleasure, relief and satisfaction fill the heart of a woman when she suckles her innocent baby. Not only that the milk starts dripping down her breasts during the period of lactation by only looking at or taking the baby in her lap. That is why such mothers are not mentioned in this Holy verse. It means that the verse is meant for both the categories of mothers mentioned above. That is why this issue has not been mentioned with its legal implications in detail[1].

---

1. The Holy Quran contains instruction from Almighty Allah which are given in a very natural and logical manner. It gives legal shape only to those things which need it. Not a single word is used in this Book which is irrelevant or unwanted. To suckle children is a generally accepted tradition in human society. This natural urge is found not only in human beings but in animals also. Almighty Allah wanted mothers to suckle their children and that is why He put it into their very nature. Consequently He thought it sufficient to command, praise and elaborate its importance only, and did not give it a legal position. It is enough to motivate a pious Muslim mother to suckle her children readily and this deed has been commended and praised in the Holy Book. It is all the more consoling to her that the Holy Messenger of Almighty Allah has given the tidings of entry to Paradise for this commendable deed. Now looking at the legal aspect of suckling one's babies whether it is commendable or obligatory, the fact is that the Holy Book has not made it a legal binding. It has not been made a compulsory duty of mothers to necessarily suckle their babies in normal conditions.

"And mothers should suckle their babies."   (2:233)

Though this verse from the Holy Quran seemingly makes it essential for mothers to suckle their babies but actually it is not so. This command is given to show that this act is liked by Almighty Allah and such mothers will earn His pleasure. Their interpretation is authenticated, by another verse from the Holy Quran which runs,

"So if they (the mothers) suckle (your babies) according to your wish give them their recompense."

This shows that suckling a child is left on the will of mothers and they are not bound to do so. Moreover, the Holy Quran has verily permitted the parents to get their babies suckled, if they so desire, by some other women with appropriate remuneration.

"But if you decide to engage a wet nurse for your children there shall be no blame on you provided you pay what you promise in fairness."

Suckling The Children and Islam

"Did bear him his mother with pain and she delivered him with pain; and bearing him and weaning him is thirty months." (46:15)

In this verse three great maternal favours have been mentioned,

(1) She carried the child during the difficult period of pregnancy.
(2) Bore the child with severe pangs of labour.
(3) Suckled the child.

These three unparalled favour from the mother make her rights over her children three times more than the father. What the Holy Book has hinted is described in detail by the Holy Prophet to one of the companions in this Hadith:

A companion asked, 'O' Messenger of Allah, who deserves my nice behaviour most?" He replied," your mother." The person then asked. "Who after her?" Again he replied, "Your mother." The man asked the same question for the third time and was replied, "your father." (Agreed upon and quoted by Riyad-Al-Sualeheen).

Since Islam is the natural religion it does not make unreasonable demands upon anyone. Generally mothers should suckle their babies for full two years. But due to some unavoidable circumstances, babies can be weaned even earlier.

> But here it should be taken into consideration that what are the motives of getting the child suckled by some other women instead of the mother herself, and whether these motives are in accordance with the Islamic laws. Moreover serious consideration should be given to the rationality of the motives through which a mother declines to suckle her baby herself. Here it should also be kept in mind that there is much difference in the properties of mother's milk and that of anyone else.

Ailing and weak mothers are also allowed not to suckle their babies. But denying the right of the child to be suckled without any fair and potent reason is unfair and unjust and below the dignity of a mother.

Mothers who do not suckle their children due to fear of being deformed and loss of their beauty and shape, are no doubt the most ruthless ones who do not deserve to be called mothers. There is no alternative to the milk of mother. The Holy Prophet has reprimanded and warned such heartless women against the terrible punishment to be meted out to them by Almighty Allah. Describing the events of the Night of Ascension he narrated:

> "Then (they), took me further ahead and I saw some women whose breasts were being continuously bitten by the snakes. On asking about the identity of these women I was told that those were the women who did not suckle their children." (Targhib-o-Tarheed)

Religious and Ethical importance of Mother's milk

Mother's milk is the natural food for a baby. It gives the baby natural health and energy. It is a spiritual and ethical nourishment too. It deeply affects the whole personality of the child. She not only provides best nourishment to the child but also infuses, with every drop of her milk, her own patterns of thinking and attitudes into his veins. It is a bare fact that food affects human attitudes and behaviours. Thus milk, being the basic food of human beings, is a matter of more importance and far-reaching consequences. Due to unfavourable conditions, if a wet nurse is to be engaged for an infant, care should be taken that she is free from any physical or mental disease and bears a

Suckling The Children and Islam

good moral character. This judicious selection will play an important role in the development of a balanced personality of the child.

Suckling the child plays a very important role in making the mother love their children deeply. This is the reason why they are always prepared to make whatever sacrifices the time and the circumstances require for their children. Mothers who do not suckle their children deliberately will not get proper love, affinity and regard from them, because they did not transfer their milk in their veins. These children could not feel the soothing and invigorating warmth of their mother's lap while the suckling the elixire of life from their breast. Naturally these children are not supposed to have the inner and spiritual attachment with their mothers.

According to the Islamic law suckling the child is a very important matter. Islam has framed various laws on its basis. In Arabic suckling the children is called Rada'at. Islam has made it a potent base for mother-child relationship. If a woman other than the mother, suckles a child, she nearly becomes his mother. This relationship is not only limited to the woman concerned but her husband and her children also attain the status of father, brothers and sisters respectively. In English they are called foster mother, foster brother and foster sister. They cannot marry among each other. According to the Holy Quran:

"And (forbidden to you are) your foster mothers and your sisters." (4:23)

It means that all the restrictions imposed on real relations also apply to foster mothers, brothers and sisters. The Holy Prophet has said:

> "Allah has forbidden relations between persons related to each other by Rada'at (suckling) like those who are related by blood." (Sahih Muslim)

This relationship is given so much importance by Islam that if two foster persons unknowingly, get married they are commanded to get separated without losing a single moment after they are aware of the fact.

Hazrat Aqaba-bin-Haris married a woman. Afterwards a woman came to the couple and told them that she had suckled both of them. He tried to ascertain it from the relatives of his wife but they expressed their ignorance about that. At last he went to the Holy Prophet and narrated the matter to him. After hearing the case the Holy Prophet asked Hazrat Aqabah to divorce his wife. He obeyed and the woman then married someone else. (Sahih Bukhari)

Reward for Suckling Mothers

In view of the extraordinary importance physical and socio-psychological benefits, the Holy Prophet has sternly warned the mothers who do not suckle their children without any potent reason, against its dire consequences. On the other hand he has advised them to do so with the tidings of being fairly rewarded here and Hereafter by Almighty Allah. He told them:

> "And for the first sip of her milk which she gives to her child, the mother gets the reward equivalent to giving life to a person." (Knaz-al-Ummal)

Moreover he has equalled a suckling mother to a dutiful warrior who vigorously guards the frontiers and she will achieve the status of a martyr if she dies during this period.

Suckling The Children and Islam

Medical and Psychological Importance of Mother's Milk

Mother's milk is extremely beneficial if viewed through its medical and psychological aspects. Experts in these fields have written a lot about it. Here some excerpts, selected from research works published by a well known medical institution, are quoted:

> "Demands of modern civilization are making us to contravene the laws of nature. Many a women do not like to suckle their children. For their information it is declared that there is no substitute to the mother's milk. If you want to save your children from different sorts of allergies and stomach disorders like stomach-ache, indigestion, diarrhoea or dysentry you should give them your own milk. After childbirth the body of the mother regains its original shape when she suckles the baby and fulfils the demands of nature. Even the twins and the children of premature birth get proper nourishment and energy for their survival, by suckling the milk of their mothers."

Medical Opinion on Mother's Milk

In the developed countries where mothers are avoiding the suckle their children due to their strange notions of modernism and emancipation, the standard of physical and mental health is falling.

After child birth the mother's milk contains colostrum for some days. This important substance immensely helps the baby grow as it contains vitamin A in abundance. But after a particular period colostrum loses this valuable vitamin. Avoidance of suckling the child right from the beginning will deprive him of this vitamin which will result in the deficient growth. Besides, colostrum also helps babies resist external infection to which they are exposed and susceptible.

The new born babies are usually exposed to the infection of the lungs and the throat. They often develop pneumonia or Diphtheria etc. In their early stages of life which might prove fatal for them. But if they go on getting colostrum in sufficient quantity they develop resistence to such deadly infections. The infants who die during the first month of their birth are usually found to be deficient of this important substance.

Modern Research

Scholars, researchers and physicians the world over agree that mother's milk is the best food for an infant which keeps them healthy and guards them against various diseases. It is the elixir for their lives. It is seen in the mammals as well as in the human beings that their own milk is best suited for their suckling. For instance cow's milk is best suited for its calves as they need quick physical growth to use their four legs for their sustenance and survival. Their mental growth is not so important as the physical one. But in human beings the infants do not need that much physical energy which is needed for the mammals as they are not required to walk and look for their own sustenance. On the contrary human babies require first the speedy development of their mental faculties and the nervous system so that they could digest, sleep, feel, understand and speak normally. Mother's milk sufficiently caters to these needs of an infant in

Suckling The Children and Islam

an efficient and natural way. That is why the babies who are fed with the cow's milk usually suffer from constipation or diarrhoea Mother's milk contains 4 % fats, while the milk of a seal (mammal-fish) has 40 % more fats as compared to that of a human mother. This is due to the fact that seal, immediately after her birth, requires a layer of fat beneath her skin to resist the ice cold waters. On the contrary a very high rate of proteins is found in the milk of a female rabbit. It is ten times more than in the human milk. For this reason their suckling grow faster. Their weight becomes double than the day they were born within six days of their birth, while a human baby normally requires six months to be double of the weight since the day they were born. Such are the laws of nature. It is surprising to note that now a days even the infants are suffering from the arterial diseases of the heart. But the children who are suckled by their mothers remain safe from such diseases.

Avoidance of Suckling the Children and Heart Diseases

According to modern research in medical field it is found out that hypertension or high blood pressure gets its roots during the period of infancy and childhood. One of the most potent causative factor of this condition is the fair amount of sodium which is found in the cow's milk. During the past ten years nearly half of the American mothers are feeding their children with cow's milk instead of their own. In a British city only thirty six out of every hundred mothers are suckling their babies. In five years fifty one percent babies have been devoid of mother's milk. These statistics are enough to disclose the reason due to which the rate of heart ailments is increasing day by day in these and such other so called modern and civilized Western countries. In fact Nature has made mother's milk best suited for their infants.

Psychological Importance of Suckling the Children

Apart from the physical importance of suckling the children, its psychological effects are also far-reaching and most beneficial for the sucklings. The child who sucks the milk of his mother in her lap not only gets the best nourishment but also feels secured. This sense of security makes the child a man or a woman of a normal and balanced personality. Lack of this priceless feeling lays the foundations of personality disturbances and such children usually become psychological patients who either find refuge in mental hospitals or become juvenile delinquents and then hardened criminals.

Psychologists, psychiatrists and sociologists the world over are of the opinion that the detrimental and rapid increase in behaviour disorders and psychological diseases are mainly due to lack of love, care and affection for children from their parents. Modern parents, particularly the mothers who are busy in economical pursuits, do not have enough time to make their children feel secured through their love, care and affection. Consequently these children get rebellious and being harbouring the feelings of hate and revenge towards their busy parents. On the other hand the conscience of such mothers often pricks them that they are doing injustice to their children by neglecting them. The feeling of guilt often makes them neurotic. Thus both the categories of such mothers and children not only lose the pleasures of their own lives but also add to the score of socio-psychological problems of their society.

Maintenance of Children

Though, according to our belief, Almighty Allah is the only Sustainer, but He has created means and sources through which this task is accomplished. Bearing the expenses of children is the second important part of their cherishment. Almighty Allah has ascribed this job to the father. Men have been selected for this job due to their physical strength and undaunted courage. Men and women both have been equipped with different capabilities to be used for different purpose. Women, soft natured, kind-hearted and patient are meant to look after their homes and their children. While men, strong, sturdy, tough, persistent and shrewd, have been allocated the responsibility of earning money to provide, sustenance for their dependents.

Meaning of Maintenance of Children

Maintenance means bearing all the expenses of a child from his birth till his adulthood, by the father. It is the religious as well as the legal responsibility of the father to meet the expenditure involved in the birth, feeding, clothing, education, health and other things relating to each and every aspect of cherishment of the child. Moreover, if he can afford, he has also to pay the amount of Sadaqa-i-Fitr and perform Aqeeqa.

Attitude of Father in the Maintenance of Children

It seems surprising that the father fulfils this responsibility with pleasure and magnanimity. He wants to provide to the best of his ability for all the needs of his children, and feels extreme sorrow and gloomy when he is unable to fulfil their wishes. He dedicates his whole life to earn and spend for the necessities and comforts of his children. He is the only man on earth who sincerely wants to see his children better off than him.

But it is not surprising at all, because Almighty Allah has saturated the heart of the father with the feelings of love, care and sacrifice of his children. Had it not been the case, things would altogether have been different. Who else would have been prepared to take so much pains to cherish and look after the needs of his children? They would have been an unwanted burden upon the society if there were a society at all. Actually this is the greatest favour from Almighty Allah that He has created natural love and affection in the hearts of parents for their children who develop the feelings of love, reverence and gratitude for their parents in turn. And thus human society is surviving and running systematically in an organized way.

Islamic Concept of the Maintenance of Children

Though a Muslim father provides financial help to his children out of his natural love for them, but at the same time he believes it to be his religious duty too. He fully knows that Almighty Allah has given them to him to be cherished and looked after in proper manner. So he not only gets pleasure and satisfaction by providing for their sustenance but also hopes that he would by rewarded by the Creator for fulfilling this duty in the life Hereafter. Hazrat Abu Masood Al-Badari Quotes a Hadith:

"When a person spends upon his wife and children with

a view to please Almighty Allah and get rewarded in Hereafter then this expenditure is taken by Allah as Sadaqah." (Riad-ul-Suahleen)(P-152)

While doing a good deed one should not have any other motive other than to earn the pleasure of Almighty Allah who might reward him in Hereafter. Otherwise any virtuous act loses its virtue and importance both.

An Example of the Holy Prophet

When Hazrat Ibrahim, the youngest son, was born to the Holy Prophet, the good news was brought to him by his servant Abu Rafey. Hazrat Mohammad (P.B.U.H.) was happy and set one slave free on this auspicious occasion. On the seventh day after the birth of the child Aqeeqah was performed and the head of the child was shaved. He gave in alms silver equivalent to the weight of the hair of the child to the poor, to please Almighty Allah.

Several women from the Ansars offered to suckle the child. He selected Kholah, the daughter of Zaid Ansari for this purpose. In recompense he gave her some date trees.

Aqeeqah

Aqeeqah is a Sunnah. It means that the Holy Prophet has done it himself and advised his followers to do it as well. But is not to be performed compulsorily. It is commendable but not essential. Those who can afford should better perform it. This is a Sadaqah (Compensation) for the life of a child. The child remains safe from different sorts of calamities by its virtue. Our Holy Prophet said:

> "Every child is mortgaged against his Aqeeqah. On the seventh day of his birth an animal should be slaughtered for him, he should be named and his/her head should be shaved the same day." (Tirmizi)

Actually Aqeeqah means that animal which is slaughtered on the seventh day of the birth of a child as a Sadaqah. If possible two goats should be slaughtered for a boy and one for a girl. But it is not necessary to slaughter two goats for a boy. One will also serve the purpose if two are not possible. But, for the affluent ones, it is better to slaughter two animals for this is the price which they have to pay for the safety of their sons and daughters. Hazrat Ali-bin-Abi-Talib quotes the saving of the Holy Prophet:

> "The Messenger of Allah slaughtered a goat for the Aqeeqah of Hazrat Hasan and said, O Fatimah get his head shaved and give in alms the silver equivalent to the weight of the hairs. We weighed his hair which were equal to or a bit lesser than a Dirham."

The ideal time for Aqeeqah is the seventh day from the birth of a child. If not possible it should be done on the fourteenth or twenty first day. It can be done whenever possible but the day should be the seventh in order of the birth of the child. It should be kept in mind that Aqeeqah is a Sunnah and it should be performed in simple manner. It is a sacred religious act and not an occasion to be celebrated with pomp and show. Some people celebrate it lavishly with music and other extravagant festivities to appease their vanity and sense of superiority. Thus they deceive themselves as well as commit a sin as Almighty Allah has commanded us never to be extravagant. By doing so they sure make a mockery of the sacred Sunnah of the Holy

Maintenance of Children

Prophet and thus become deserving case for the punishment from Him and also cause pain and sorrow to the departed soul of the Holy Prophet.

Circumcision

Circumcision is an act done by all the Messengers of Almighty Allah as well as an Islamic principle. Hazrat Abu Hurairah relates that the Holy Prophet once said:

> "Human decency consists of five acts: to get circumcised (by men), to do away with the pubic hair, to do away with the hair under the armpits, to cut the moustaches and to clip ones nails."

Actually these are five basic acts of personal hygiene Decency and civilization demand that we have to do these acts. These may be called instinctive behaviour of man which has been given to mankind by the Creator to be the best of all the creatures in the world. This is the practice of all the prophets and all of them have instructed their followers to do so. If the male baby is of normal health, it is better to circumcise him on the seventh day of his birth. It has two-fold benefits. Firstly the skin of the child, at this time, is soft and gets healed up soon. Secondly this act would also get the sanctity of following the Sunnah of the Holy Prophet who has hinted that it should be done on the seventh day. Hazrat Salman-bin-Amir once heard the Messenger of Allah saying:

> "Birth of a child and Aqeeqah go together, so spill blood (sacrificial slaughter) on his behalf and take away fifth from him or her."(Bukhari)

By 'taking away the filth' means giving bath and shaving the head of the infant after birth. Some religious scholars have included the circumcision in these steps towards purifying the child, as it also adds to the personal cleanliness. Therefore it is best to get the male child circumcised on the seventh day of his birth. If unable to do so due to some compelling circumstances they should do it within forty days therefrom. After these two initial periods the following points should be taken care of. Firstly it should definitely be done not later than the seventh years of the age of the child, because after this age the skin gets thicker and circumcision becomes more painful. Secondly this Sunnah should be followed in very simple and frugal manner. It should not be given the shape of a festivity or pompous celebration. To be extravagant on such occasion will lose its religious aspect and will prove a burdensome responsibility for those who cannot afford it that way. Simple and modest rejoicing with limited number of relatives and friends is however permissible. But it makes it a sin rather than a virtue if done otherwise.

Hazrat Usman-bin-Abi-Al-Aas was invited to the celebration of the circumcision of a child. He did not accept the invitation. When asked the reason for the refusal he replied, "In the days of Holy Prophet, neither we were invited to such celebrations nor we participated."

Recompense for Suckling the Children

Recompense for the women who suckles the children is to be paid by the father. If the husband has divorced the wife or vice versa then it is better that the child should be suckled by the mother. The mother should also not deprive the child of her milk which is the right of the child. It is the duty of the father in such cases that he should bear the expenses of the mother of the child without fail. If due to some unfavourable conditions the mother is unable to suckle her child or the father due to

Maintenance of Children

some reasons of his own, wants to get the child suckled by some other women, it is the religious duty of the father to bear all the expenses of that woman. In case the father dies during this period, the grandfather of the child or his guardian has to pay the recompense to the woman concerned. According to the Holy Quran:

> "And the mothers shall suckle their children for full two years. If (the father) desires to complete the term of suckling; and on the father shall be their sustenance and their clothing in fairness; burdened not is any soul save to (the extent of) his (individual) ability; neither shall a mother be made suffer (any difficulty or loss) on account of her child nor a father because of his child, and (if the father be not there) on the heir (of the father) devolves a similar responsibility; and if both (the father and mother) decide on weaning, by mutual consent and (with due consultation) there shall be no blame on them; But if you decide to engage a wet nurse for your children there shall be no blame on you provided you promise in fairness; and fear Allah and know that Allah sees what you do." (2:233)

The Ayah contains seven basic principles about suckling the child:

1. Normally mothers should suckle their children two years.
2. Mothers who are separated from the fathers of their children should also suckle their children in cases fathers want them to do so.
3. During the period of suckling the child and mother's personal expenses should be borne by the father of the child.

4. In case of the absence of father the paternal grand-father or the guardian of the child has to pay the recompense to the suckling woman.

5. There should be no exploitation from either side. Neither the father should pay unfairly to the mother thinking that she is compelled by her natural urge and love to suckle her child, nor the wife should demand unfair payment from the father. It should be a fair deal from both the sides.

6. If the father and mother agree by mutual consultation they can wean out the baby even before two years.

7. If for any reason, the mother does not want to suckle the child or the father does not wish to get the child suckled by his mother, a wet nurse can be arranged. But the payment should be settled by mutual consent in advance according to the prevailing conditions.

These principles are not meant only for recitation, but should be practiced properly. And this can be done only by those who fear Allah and believe that He is always watching them.

Maintenance of Children According to the Holy Quran

Though the sustainment of children is not mentioned pointedly in the Holy Quran but it does not mean that it has been skipped altogether. In fact the Holy Quran is the most comprehensive Book which contains each and every thing concerning the life of man. In fact the Quran depicts its laws in a most wise manner having due consideration for human feelings and psychology. Sustainment of children is such an acknowledged accredited and natural pattern of human behaviour that it was not considered to be mentioned as a separate commandment by Almighty Allah in His Holy Book. But he did refer to it in a very judicious, compact and logical way.

According to the Quranic verse quoted earlier, the father will be responsible for bearing the expenses of the woman whom he wants to suckle his child. In case of the absence of the father the suckling woman is to be compensated by the paternal grandfather of the child. Thus Almighty Allah has made the father responsible for bearing the expenses of an unrelated woman for the obvious reason that she has suckled the child. She as a right to be maintained by the father for her services to the child. It is beyond common sense that a man be held responsible for the maintenance of the woman who suckle his child yet he remains free from the responsibility of the sustainment of his child for whom all these commandments stand. Whatever he gives to the woman concerned in token of her services, he gives for the benefit of his own child. It proves that the father is held responsible for the maintenance of his child. And this logical connotation of the Holy Quran in elaborated by the Holy Prophet in details.

Maintenance of Children According to Hadith

All aspects of this issue have been elaborated by the Holy Prophet in details. Muslims should keep in mind all these aspects in order to maintain their children properly and in tune with the requirements of Islam.

Foremost Duty

The children come first in order of priority to be benefited from the earnings of their parents. It is not only a worldly affair but a religious duty too. Islam, has advised the parents to meet the requirements of their children first. Even the alms and the charity come next to it. To give alms or charity to the extent that one's children may be affected and their needs may remain unmet is disliked by Almighty Allah and His Holy Prophet. It is sheer ignorance on the part of the parents to spend for the vanity and vainglory while their own children are not properly maintained. The children even after divorce are the first and foremost beneficiaries of the earnings of their parents. The Holy Prophet has advised the parents to do so in the following words, "The best charity is that which leaves you financially secured. Spend first on those whose maintenance is your responsibility."

(Bukhari, quoted in Mishkat)

This Hadith provides a balanced, normal and natural point of view. Everybody desires his children to be benefitted and comforted by whatever he has and live a comfortable life. It is also the most potent motive to earn and save or invest money. Generally it is seen that we try to make more and more money in order to maintain our children well and also to leave behind as much as we possibly can for them. Islam gives considerable importance to spending upon the poor, so much so that it is placed as one of the basic requirements of Faith. On the other hand our religion condemns miserliness and pronounces it, as a sign of hypocrisy. But it equally commands us first to look after the needs of those who are to be maintained by us. It clearly shows that charity at the cost of the maintenance of children is not at all wanted by Islam. Best charity is that which does not leave the children as destitutes.

Negligence of Maintaining the Children

Avoiding the parental duty of maintaining the children is a serious sin in the eyes of Almighty Allah. According to Hadith,

Maintenance of Children

"It is quite sufficient to make one a sinner that he is neglecting his dependents." (Riyaz-al-Sualeheen, Abu Dwood etc.)

It is clear from the above Hadith that it is enough for one to earn the wrath of Almighty Allah and be a sinner to neglect the maintenance of those who are made his dependents. There can be several aspects of this negligence by a father:

1. Spending for the show & vanity but ignoring the rights of family members.

2. Spending on his own pleasure and comfort but starving the children.

3. Spending in giving alms and charity while depriving the children of their requirements due to ignorance of Islamic principles.

4. Starving the children by being lazy and sluggish and unwilling to work hard to earn more.

However, whatever the case may be, maintenance of children is the religious responsibility of every father. Carelessness and avoidance of this responsibility is a grave sin.

The Most Rewarding Expenditure

Hazrat Abu Hurairah quotes the Holy Prophet to have said: "If you spend your Dinar one in the way of Allah, one to free a slave, one as charity to the poor and one on your family and children, then out of all these four Dinars the most rewarding one is that which you spent on your children. (Sahih Muslim).

Another Hadith elaborates it further which is narrated by Hazrat Sauban.:

> "The most sovereign (gold coin) is that which is spent for one's family and children, the one which is spent on animals for (Jihad) in the way of Allah, the one spent on the comrades in the way of Allah.
>
> "Abu Qulabah-one of the narrators says that the Holy Prophet began saying from spending on one's children and then said,
>
> "Who can be the most deserving person to be rewarded (by Almighty Allah) than the one who spends on his children so that they may be saved from begging and may prosper." (Tirmizi)

The Most Fortunate Father

Hazrat Abu Hurairah narrates that the Holy Prophet said: "The person who earned lawfully, to save himself from begging and to provide for the sustenance of his family and to help his neighbour, will meet Almighty Allah on the day of judgement with the face shining like full moon. And the one who earned unlawfully with a view to get more well off than before and to show off his financial superiority over others will meet Allah in extreme anger." (Baihaqi)

The Mother Who Spends Upon Her Children

Islam has not burdened mothers with the problem of earning for the maintenance of children. This job has been entrusted to fathers only. This demarcation of the fields of both father and

Maintenance of Children

mother was necessary so that both may put in their best efforts and fulfil their duties satisfactorily in their respective fields. But it does not mean that if a mother who spends upon the maintenance of her children will not be rewarded by Almighty Allah. In cases where husbands are dead or poorly paid or invalid, the wives who earn for maintainery their childern will definitely be rewarded by Him. Hazrat Umm-i-Salmah narrates that once she asked the Holy Prophet;

> "Shall I be rewarded (by Almighty Allah) for spending upon the sons of Abu Salmah? I cannot leave them in want and hunger wandering like beggars from door to door. After all they are my sons."

> "The Holy Prophet of Almighty Allah replied "Yes, you will definitely be rewarded (by Almighty Allah) for what ever you will spend on them."   (Riyaz al-Sualeheen)

Umm-UL-Momineu Hazrat Umm-i-Salmah had two sons and two daughters from her first husband, Hazrat Abu Salmah. She asked the above mentioned question regarding these children. This Hadith clarified two aspects for us.

Firstly, though the mother is not legally responsible for the financial maintenance of her children, but if she does so, she will surely be rewarded and recompensed by Almighty Allah.

Secondly it tells us as to what should be the attitude of true Muslim mother towards her children. Hazrat Umm-i-Salmah feels compelled by the natural love and affection for her children to cater for their needs after the death of their father, she feels it her duty to do so and proclaims.

"I cannot leave then to wander from door to door like beggars."

But at the same time she is also anxious to know whether she would be rewarded for this act by Almighty Allah in her after life. This shows that a true Muslim always keeps in mind the life hereafter and acts virtuously. He acts virtuously always with the hope of being rewarded in his real and ever lasting life which begins after death.

Sustenance Of Daughters

Islam, together with the general instructions about the sustenance of children, has given special importance to the cherishment of daughters. Pronouncing it more rewarding it has particularly induced the parents towards it.

Actually in our society the girls are considered a weaker creature. Parents think that girls are unable to help them in their hours of need. They are not even supposed to render prolonged service to the parents as they are married off as soon as they become capable of doing so. Nor they can defend their parents at a critical hour. In such circumstances those parents who are unaware of the teachings of Islam in this respect may not be able to cherish their daughters properly, and may deprive them of that love, affection and behaviour which they deserve. Therefore it is essential for all the Muslims to know these teachings about the cherishment of daughters well and practice them in their daily lives without fail.

The Enviable Reward

Hazrat Anas narrates that the Holy Prophet said:

"One who cherished two daughters till they were major (and married off) will be so near with me on the last day, like these two fingers and then he showed the two fingers joining them together."

Muslim Parents

How fortunate will be the parents who will have the honour of having the company of our beloved Prophet on the Last day.

The Mothers Who Deserve Heaven

Hazrat Aisha relates,

" A poor woman came to me with her two daughters, I gave her three dates, she gave two dates, one each to her two daughters and wanted to eat the remaining one herself but her daughters asked the third one too. The mother then distributed the date in two equal parts and gave them one part each instead of eating it herself. I was very much impressed by this maternal love and I told the matter to the Holy Prophet. He said,

"This act of sacrifice for her daughters has made her the sure entrant in Heaven and has saved her from the fire of Hell."

A Daughter - Heaven for Parents

The parents of a daughter are indeed lucky. It means that Almighty Allah has made them caretakers for their Heaven - their daughter. Now it is completely upto them to get it or lose it. The Holy Prophet has given the clear tidings that parents who cherished their daughters in a befitting manner would undoubtedly get their abodes in Paradise. That is why the parents of a daughter are really the most fortunate ones. Hazrat Jabir-bin-Abdullah narrates that once the Prophet of Allah said:

"One who has three daughters and guards them, caters to their needs and remains kind towards them will surely

Sustenance of Daughters

get Heaven. Some one asked him about one who had only two daughters. The Holy Prophet said, even then."
(Al-Adab-al-Mufrad)

There is also a similar narration in Mishkat which is narrated by Abdullah-bin-Abbas. He said that the Holy Prophet would have given the same tidings even in case of parents who had only one daughter.

Warding a Destitute Daughter

The Holy Prophet said: shall I not tell you the best charity. It is the daughter, returned to you and there is none else to take care of her except you." (Ibn Majah)

Here, the destitute daughter is no doubt that who has returned to her parents after divorce, separation or being a widow. But it also pertains to a daughter who remains unmarried due to some physical or mental handicap. This treatment of parents with such a daughter is highly pleasing to Almighty Allah. For this reason warding a destitute daughter is described by the Holy Prophet as the best charity.

The Revolutionary Change

The revolutionary teachings of Islam brought miraculous changes in the thinking and behaviour of the pagan Arabs so rapidly that it is rightly considered as a golden chapter of the History. These pleasant and auspicious changes would have been seen and enjoyed by those fortunate persons who belonged to that age—those who had seen the difference between the pre-Islamic period and the period after the advent of Islam with their own eyes. But even today one can be elated and thrilled by the magnificence and grandeur of that blessed period by turning the pages of Arab History.

In the pre-Islamic Arabia, it was a matter of pride for a father to be cruel and hard hearted towards his daughter. He would prefer her death than her existence. A poet of that period says,

> "She prays for a long life for me and I, out of sheer love, wish her dead, for the best befitting thing for her is death."

Another poet proclaims:

> "In fact women are satans who are created for us. May God save us from the treachery of these satan."

When the daughter of the chief of Bahrah breathed her last Abu Bakr Kharzmi wrote the following letter of condolence to the father of the deceased,

> "Even you are grieved by recollecting the modesty and other qualities of the deceased it is better to congratulate you, rather than offering the condolences. This is due to the fact that the things which are to be secluded should better be hidden for ever. The most honourable things is to bury the daughters alive. We are passing through the age in which blessed is the man whose wife dies before him. And if he buried his daughter with his own hands, he no doubt has taken full revenge from his son-in law."

Sustenance of Daughters

Qais-bin-Asim, the chief of the tribe of Banu-Tameem once confessed to the Holy Prophet that he had buried his ten daughters alive by his own hands. Another fellow described a similar incident in such a pathetic way before the Holy Messenger that it made him weep. Thus we can clearly visualise that inhuman and heinous traditions and customs were rampant among Arabs during the pre-Islamic period.

But after the advent of Islam the same Arab society underwent a revolutionary change through absorbing the teachings of Islam. The very existence of a daughter, which once was a stigma of shame and indignation, became a source of pride and deliverance for the parents. Persons who once used to snatch away the daughters from the laps of their mothers for burying them alive now started to prevail upon one another to cherish the daughters of others.

An Interesting Scene

While on his way back to Medina after performing Umrah at Mecca an orphan girl came running towards the Holy Prophet crying "uncle, O' uncle". This girl was Hazrat Hamza's daughter who was left in Mecca. Seeing her, Hazrat Ali took the child in his arms and gave her to Hazrat Fatimah saying, "Take her, she is your uncle's daughter". Then followed a pleasant altercation between the persons present there. Hazrat Jafar requested the Holy Prophet to handover the girl to him as his wife was the girl's aunt (mother's sister). Hazrat Zaid proved his claim over the child by pleading that the father of the girl was just like his real brother. Hazrat Ali who had the girl already in his arms claimed her guardianship by saying, "O' Holy Prophet this girl should be mine as she is my sister. Moreover she was first picked up by me". The beloved Messenger of Almighty Allah was moved by such an emotional scene. He pondered over the situation and then decided that the girl should be given to her aunt and added that, "Aunt is the best substitute for her mother."

During these days daughters were so much loved, valued and respected that a pagan poet satirically said: "After the prophethood of Muhammad (peace be upon him) there are girls and girls everywhere."

Pleasant Behaviour

The third right of the children is that their parents should treat them with love and affection. They should be kind, sympathetic and reasonable to their children. The parents should do their best possible to keep their children happy and satisfied. They should avoid any such attitude which injures their feelings, ego or self-respect.

Your little children are your wards and your dependent. Till a certain age they have none but you - their parents - to look after them and fulfill their needs. Almighty Allah has blessed you with children. They are boons from Him for you. Be thankful for this precious favour and valued them with all the care and affection you possibly can offer to them. Treat them with love and affection which they deserve.

Almighty Allah has given you children as a trust. You are their trustees and their protectors, you have to take extreme care that you try your best to prepare and equip them with all the skill and capabilities which they require to pass their lives in tune with the time and circumstances in which they have to live. They should be the harbingers of fame and respect for you as well as for their own selves in this world and hereafter.

Results of Maltreatment with the Children

The unfair treatment with the children is injurious and harmful equally for the parents, the children and the societies. One of the most intriguing social problems of advanced societies and to a certin extent in our own society too—is the strained and antagonistic relations of the adolescent children with their parents and elders. One of the major casual factors of this perplexing problem is the wrong attitude of parents with their children during their infancy and even hereafter.

Harsh and overstrict attitude like scolding, abusing, calling names and blaming them for the assumed faults and other such behaviour with children injures and mutilates their ego. It makes them nervous, psychologically disturbed and rebellious. They start harbouring the feelings of hate and revenge for such parents and then for the whole society. Most of them become insolent, rue and rebellious and never hesitate to make their parents sorrowful by their misdeeds and mischiefs whenever they get a chance to do so. Later on they turn into juvenile delinquents and become a menace for their parents as well as for the whole society. At last they become hardened criminals and make the jails and prisons their home and the society their field of their criminal and disastrous operations.

Children, by nature, need love and affection from their parents. If they do not get it in their home they try to get it from outside. When they come out they come across other such

Muslim Parents

children who welcome them and from a group of their own where they get what they needed. Some of them who cannot even adjust them anywhere, ultimately, land in lunatic asylums and mental hospitals. However, in any case such homes are the miniature replica of Hell where things like peace, pleasure, satisfaction and homeliness are unimaginable.

A Revealing Incident

Once the author asked a young man as to why was he not maintaining pleasant relationship with his parents. Being near to me he told the following story:

> "My father is a callous, overstrict and aggressive type of man. Since my childhood I was always afraid of him. Due to his aggressive attitude I tried my best to avoid him for fear of chiding, criticism and rebuking by him. In the night, before going to sleep, I was always put to every type of humiliation and indignation for my faults which happened throughout the day. In the morning I woke up prepared for the same treatment again. It was the rarest and the luckiest day of my life during which I was scolded two or three times only. I anxiously awaited him going out and intensely dreaded his presence in the house. Whenever I came across the boys whose fathers were kind and tender to them I envied them and wished that I had such a father too. In such circumstances how could I be otherwise"?

The terrible story still rings in my ears.. From the story we can still understand the importance and responsibility of a father.

Sustenance of Daughters

If the parents want to see their children having balanced personalities and normal relations with them, they must be careful of their own behaviour and treatment with their children. Children, by nature, are not lifeless pieces of chess which you can move anywhere and anytime of your own sweet will. They have got their own psychology and they have to be dealt with accordingly. Their whole personality is formed according to the environment they get in their homes.

Misbehaviour of parents with their children mutilates their ego and self-respect. We all have the natural desire to be loved. Particularly the children need it badly because upto a certain age they need help and guidance in most of their matter. When, instead of love, care and affection, they receive ridicule, rebukes, criticism and harshness their whole personalities go to pieces. They lose the meanings of the conceptions like love, tenderness, self confidence, courage, self respect and other such moral attitudes. Rather they become rude, rebellious, short-tempered, narrow-minded, shy and start suffering from inferiority and other psychological complexes. In short their whole lives are torn to pieces and they no longer remain normal persons.

Consequently the parents should take their relationship with their children as a matter of mutual 'give and take'. They should treat their children exactly the way they want themselves to be treated by them. First they will learn the ways of nice and normal behaviour from the patterns set by their parents and will treat them with the same attitude when their turn comes. Only then your children will be happy and satisfied with you and they would sincerely pray to Almighty Allah.

Muslim Parents

"O' Lord have mercy upon my parents as they cherished me with love and kindness in my infancy and childhood".

(17:24)

The Holy Quran and the Parental Behaviour

Almighty Allah, in His Holy Book, stresses upon the parents to treat their children with love, affection and forgiveness. He dislikes the parents who adopt harsh, aggressive and revengeful attitude towards their children who commit minor mistakes. He forgives and has mercy upon them only who treat their children and other members of the family with kindness and compassion.

"And if you forgive, overlook and cover up (the ills of your wives and children) then verily Allah is Oft Forgiving, the most merciful". (64:14)

Some persons who embraced Islam could not migrate to Medina with the Holy Prophet. This happened due to the strong resistance from their family members who tolerated their acceptance of Islam but could not allow their departure from them. They yielded to this emotional pressure and postponed Hijrah. When, later, they reached Medina they were pained to see that those who had migrated earlier were far ahead of them in the field of learning and advancement. They felt that it was all due to the resistence from their wives and children against the migration. Being furious at this, they intended to take revenge and punish their dependents. On this occasion the Holy Prophet advised them not to do so as it were they themselves who made this decision and preferred to concede to their demands. In future they were advised to beware of them and warned that Almighty Allah never likes those who become rude, punish or avenge their members of the family. Islam demands you to be kind to them as Almighty Allah Himself is Most Forgiving and likes those who forgive. He is most benevolent and likes those who are kind to others. Those who want Almighty Allah to be kind and forgiving to them, they must treat their children with love and kindness and forgive them readily for their shortcomings.

The Holy Prophet on Nice Treatment with Children

The Messenger of Allah has elaborately discussed about various aspects of the behaviour of parents with their children. He has vividly told about the reward and benefit, herein and hereafter, and clearly indicated towards the ideological and practical errors about this important issue for the guidance of parents. He regulated the parental behaviour so that any of the parties may not be aggrieved. Following is the Hadith which stresses equal treatment with the children,

> "Noman-bin-Basheer relates that his father gave him a gift. His mother Umrah, daughter of Rawaha said that she will not approve it unless the Holy Prophet be a witness to it. He, accordingly went to the Messenger of Almighty Allah and told him the matter. The Holy Prophet asked him whether he had given the same gift to all of his children? To this he answered in the negative. On hearing this the Holy Prophet told him to fear

Muslim Parents

Almighty Allah and do justice with his children. He then, came back home and cancelled the gift. According to another version of this the Holy Prophet told the father of Noman that he could not be witness of cruelty".

(Bukhari, Muslim)

According to the third version of this Hadith the Holy Prophet asked Noman, "Do you want to be treated by your children all alike". Noman replied in the affirmation. The Holy Prophet then said, "Then you should not do like this (injustice)."

No doubt it is very difficult to love his children in an exactly equal manner. Exactness and equality in love for more than one person is merely impossible for human beings and that is why those are not demanded in the above quoted Hadith. What the Holy Prophet has demanded of the parents is that their treatment should be equal and just with all their children. For them all their children are equal and so should they behave with them too. There is no difference in the rights of children. They all enjoy equal rights upon their parents. Consequently the parents are asked to avoid prejudiced and different behaviour with them.. Parent's different and prejudiced behaviour entails social as well as psychological handicaps for their children. In the first place through their unequal and imbalanced attitude they are denying the rights of other children. This is unsocial, immoral and improper. Secondly this uncalled for and biased attitude creates grave psychological disturbances and makes the mal-treated child feel inferior to the rest of the children. On the other hand the children who are given preferential treatment start and continue

Sustenance of Daughters

their authoritative behaviour with their unequally treated brothers and sisters. With the passage of time such children start hating and avoiding each other which ultimately makes far away each other. Throughout their lives they live like rivals and thus leave these feelings of antagonism and enmity in the hearts of their children. So the preferential treatment of parents with their children make them enemies instead of brothers and sisters. Apart from such rueful situations another damage is done which is irreparable and injurious to the society. The image of such parents is also impaired and their children who do not get equal treatment from them, lose the feelings of respect and reverence for them. Such children in their heart of hearts, hate these parents who have treated them with less or no love in comparison with their other sisters or brothers.

Sometimes in the cases of death or divorce, parents do not treat their step-children with the same love and affection as they treat their own. Often the children of new wife or husband are better treated while the children of former spouses are neglected. In the cases where parents do not like or love their step-children due to their faulty behaviour or they are unwanted parents are helpless. But even then Islam requires them to treat all the children fairly and equally. One can justify his wrong and faulty behaviour and deceive his own conscience by lame and self-invented excuses but he can never hide anything from Almighty Allah who is the supreme knower and nothing is hidden from Him. So the parents should never exhibit preference and prejudices in their attitude towards their children. That is why the Holy Prophet termed this attitude as "cruelty" and he did not like to be a witness to an act of cruelty. Hazrat Noman was committing the same crime. He was giving a gift to his son from one wife but depriving the children from his other wife of this gift. When he was told the correct and just line of action he corrected himself and refrained from meting out preferential treatment to children.

Unequal Treatment with Sons and Daughters

Hazrat Ibn Abbas relates that the Messenger of Almighty Allah said: "the person who got a daughter and did not bury her alive neither degraded her nor gave preference to the sons against her, Almighty Allah would enter him into the Heaven." (Abu Dawood)

In this Hadith the entry of parents into Heaven depends upon three conditions which are:

1. They should not bury their daughters alive.

2. They should not degrade or insult her.

3. They should not give preference to their sons over their daughters.

As far as the first condition is concerned it is now totally abolished from Muslim society. After the dawn of Islam the Holy Prophet of Allah, through his forceful and effective teachings, this savage tradition came to an end. And now no Muslim on earth can even imagine to commit such a heinous crime. But in some Muslim families who are ignorant still neglect the last two conditions.

In such families sons are given more importance than the daughters. They are much more loved, cared for and valued than their sisters.

Sustenance of Daughters

The only reason for this biased attitude of parents towards their sons and daughters seems to be the notion that daughters are not for them. They are cherished and brought up for others who become their masters. Parents do not expect for a moment that they can be helped or benefitted, financially or otherwise by the daughters. They are mere burdens for them right from their birth till death. They think that the daughters grace others homes while sons are the source of grace for their own houses. In most of the families, the parents have high hopes and expectations of their sons as they are supposed to add their wealth and property and would support them in their old age, while their daughters will always make them spend. Consequently the sons are thought to be the assets while the daughters are considered mere liabilities for ever. This thinking motivates them to cherish their sons with pleasure and fervour while daughters do not get such treatment.

Usually daughters in our society are still unwanted and grudgingly tolerated. Sons are still preferred and parents think themselves lucky to have as many sons as they get and celebrate their birth with joy and happiness. But their faces darken with gloom and displeasure when a daughter is born to them. Parents and grand parents get a lot of congratulations from relations, neighbours, friends and acquaintances on the so called happy occasion of the birth of a boy in the family. The mother, after giving birth to a son feels proud and looks at her husband with a feeling of pride and elation. And the happy father, his eyes full of joy and exaltation acknowledges the indebtedness to his wife and she enjoys respect and sympathies of all concerned. On the other hand she feels ashamed to give birth to a daughter. An inert atmosphere of gloom shrouds the house and the poor

Muslim Parents

mother feels, rather is made to feel, that she has let down the whole family by giving birth to a daughter. On such occasion most of the people sympathise with the parents, and fallaciously enumerate the blessings of having a daughter only to console them and share their grief. So from the very birth of a son or a daughter a set pattern of behaviour is adopted in the family. Both these attitudes are different and prejudiced. In such families boys have always the upper hand over the girls. Whatever they give their daughter as dowry, at the time of their marriage, is given under compulsion and under duress just to save honour and enhance the position of their daughter in the family of their husband. They think that whatever they are giving to their daughters is going out of their house to the aliens. On the other hand, they think that their sons' wives bring the dowry to add to their fortunes. The children of their sons will be their own family assets. In short they will lose in case of daughters and get in case of their sons. Due to this attitude such parents treat their sons and daughters differently.

The above Hadith condemns such prejudicial behaviour of parents with their children and also warns Muslims that such an attitude displeases Almighty Allah. To win His pleasure and earn Paradise, parents should treat their sons and daughters equally. In no case they should adopt preferential attitude towards their children in any sphere of life. Both the male and female children should be given equal love, affection, care and importance so that they might not suffer from social and psychological hazards. They should always abide by the rules and regulations of Islam instead of adopting the unfair and unreasonable customs and their personal prejudices and preferences.

Sustenance of Daughters

A Daughter - Shield from the Fire of Hell

According to Hazrat Aisha: "A woman came to me with her two little daughters for some help. At that time I had nothing but a date. I gave her that very date to eat. She distributed it among her both the daughters and did not take it herself. The woman then went away. When the Holy Prophet came home I told him the incident. He replied that the person (mother) who was put to test through these girls and who treated them fairly would sure find these girls as shields for her from the fire of Hell".

(Riyaz-Al-Sualeheen)

A daughter may not be a source of material benefit for the parents but they will be fully benefitted in the life hereafter on the basis of their pleasant and kind behaviour to her. And this will be the most important benefit because deliverance from the fire of Hell is the most cherished and sought for desire of all the Muslims. In the light of the above quoted Hadith only the lucky ones have daughters — daughters who will spare their kind and loving parents from the most shattering agony in Hereafter. Moreover it is an undeniable fact that daughters are more loving and attentive to their parents as compared to the sons.

Reward for Kindness

It is related that a man came to the Holy Prophet with his child whom he warmly held in his arms. Seeing this the Holy Prophet asked him, "Are you doing this out of love and kindness"? The man replied in the affirmative. He then told him, "With whatever love and kindness you are treating this child you will

Muslim Parents

get the favour from Almighty Allah in a far greater degree as his kindness overrides the kindness of All His creatures".

(Al-Adab Al-Mufrad)

Behaviour of The Holy Prophet With His Children

Each and every act of the Holy Prophet has been recorded, remembered and written down by his wives, children and the companions and preserved them in the books of Hadith and prographies. Even the most minor events of his personal life are safe and sound in the books. But it is surprising to note that throughout his whole sacred life not a single incident is found about his being unkind, indifferent or even harsh to his children. Apart from being never unkind to his children he never showed indifference even to his servants. Hazrat Anas relates, "I served the Holy Prophet for ten years at Madina. At that time I was just a boy and often I was unable to serve him fully according to his requirements. But during the whole span of these ten years he never scolded me and never asked me why I did this and why I was unable to do that"? Hazrat Aisha tells about the behaviour of her loving husband in these words, "The Holy Prophet never punished any slave, male or female, woman or animal.........and whenever he entered home I found him smiling."

Behaviour of the Holy Prophet with his Daughter

The Messenger of Almighty Allah used to say about his daughter:

"Fatimah is a part of my body. One who will displease her will earn my displeasure too". (Bukhari)

Muslim Parents

After her marriage whenever she visited her Holy father, he always stood up to welcome her, kissed upon her forehead and gave her his own seat to sit. (Abu Dawood)

He loved her so deeply that whenever he would see her in a pensive mood would himself become sad and restless. Once he went to her house looking very sad. But, after some time, he came out quite gay and happy. The companions asked the reason of these changing attitudes. The Holy Prophet replied I have solved the differences and got reconciled the two persons whom I extremely love. (Tabaqat Ibne Sad)

The Holy Prophet was putting up with Hazrat Abu Ayub Ansari at Madina. The house of Hazrat Fatimah was at a little distance from there. Once the Holy Prophet went to his daughter and told her that he wanted to get a house for her near him so that the distance could be shortened. Hazrat Fatimah, in agreement, told her Holy father that Haris-Bin-Noman owned several houses and he would have no objection in giving one to her. Her pious father replied that he felt hesitation in doing that. Some how the matter came to the knowledge of Hazrat Haris. He came to the Holy Prophet and said: "O' Prophet of Almighty Allah I have heard that you want to shift your daughter in a house near you. O' Prophet of Allah, my parents may be sacrificed upon you, all these my houses are at your disposal. Bring her in any of these houses you desire. Allah be my witness that nothing will make me more happy than any of my belongings accepted and used by you". The Holy Prophet appreciated the feelings of Hazrat Haris and prayed to Almighty Allah for him and then brought her daughter in one of the houses of Hazrat Haris near him. Whenever the Holy Prophet went on a journey he always visited her daughter in the last and never departed

Behaviour of the Holy Prophet With His Children

without seeing her. In the same way, when he would return he would go to see her first after offering thanks-giving prayers.

He also loved his grand children (two sons of Hazrat Fatimah). Whenever he would go to his daughter he would say to her, bring me my sons. When they came to him he would smell them and embrace them well.

Hazrat Zainab was the eldest daughter of the Holy Prophet. She was married to her cousin Abul-As. Hazrat Khadija, on the occasion of Hazrat Zainab's marriage, gave her a locket studded with a priceless stone from Yemen. When the Holy Prophet migrated to Medina, Hazrat Zainab remained at Mecca with her husband who had not embraced Islam till then. He fought against Muslims in the battle of Badr. After the battle, which was won by the Muslims, he was brought to Medina as a prisoner of war. He sent the message to his home for paying the ransom for his release. His wife, Hazrat Zainab, sent him that very locket which was gifted to her by her mother at the time of her marriage. When the Holy Prophet saw that locket he immediately recognised it and could not control his tears. His companions who knew all the matter well, were also moved and anxious by this sight. He then asked them that if they agree, the locket may be returned to his daughter and his husband may also be set free. All the companions readily and happily agreed to the proposal. Afterwards Abul-As was released and the locket of his wife was also given back to him on the condition that he would send Hazrat Zainab to her Holy father at Madina. Abul-As honoured the promise and sent his wife to the Holy Prophet.

After some time Abul-As came to Madina and embraced Islam. Hazrat Zainab breathed her last in 8th Hijrah after fifteen

Muslim Parents

months her husband came to Madina. The Holy Prophet himself put her into the grave. At that moment he was deeply moved and stricken with grief. After laying her in the grave he prayed to Almighty Allah: "O Lord, she was too weak, O' Allah be kind to her and make her grave spacious."

(Usud-Ul-Ghaba)

Giving Good Names To The Children

The name has psychological effect upon the personality of an individual. His whole personality develops under the shadow of the meaning and impression of his name. Moreover it is obvious that we like the names which have pleasant sound effects and nice meanings. Therefore we should always take care while giving name to our children. We should give them pleasant, short and meaningful names which should easily be understood and appreciated.

Names had much importance to the Holy Prophet. He has advised his followers to give good and meaningful names, to their children. Several persons would come to him asking to suggest names for their born babies. He would always suggest fair and meaningful names to them. He would never ask the person to help him who had a meaningless and ugly name. He would like the persons who had good names, pray for them and readily let them do something for him if needed. Whenever he went out he liked to hear names like Najeeh (The successful) or Rashid (The Righteous). Whenever he entered a new town he enquired it's name and was pleased with the fair name. He would give a better one in case its name was ugly. He could not tolerate improper name of anything, be it a person, a town or a land, there was a peice of land which was called Huzrah (uneven and arid) which he changed to Khuzrah (verdurous and fertile). A valley which was called she be Zallah (The valley of Astrays).

Muslim Parents

The Holy Prophet changed it to Shebe Huda (The valley of guidance). He also changed the names of many men and women. It is also said that those who insisted upon the former names and did not adopt those suggested by the Holy Prophet remained always in trouble.

Good Names for Children

While selecting the names for children the following points should be kept in mind,

1. It should contain one of the names of Almighty Allah and should be prefixed by a word which shows submission to Him. For example, Abdullah, Abdul Rahman, Abdul Ghaffar, Amtullah, Amtul Rahman etc.

2. It should be selected from the names of the Holy Mesengers like Yaqoob, Yousuf, Idress, Ahmad, Ibraheem, Ismaeel, Muhammad etc.

3. It should be adopted from the names of holy and pious persons like Umar Farooq, Siddiq, Khalid, Ali, Usman, Khadija, Hajira, Maryam, Umm-i-Salmah, Sumayyah etc.

4. It should reflect the true Islamic spirit and thought of the parents. For instance, keeping in view the present deteriorating condition of Muslims, the child should be given the names like Tariq, Salahuddin with the hope that this child would become like the person whose name he is given.

5. Conforming to good habits, such as; Saeed (Lucky and submissive), Shafiq (Kind), Sharif (Noble) etc.

6. It's meaning should be pleasant and virtuous.

Giving Good Names To The Children

These were the things which should be adopted while giving names to the children. Now we point out some names which should be avoided.

1. It should not be against the spirit and tenets of Islam such as Abdul Rasool, etc.
2. It should not reflect the bad habits like pride, haughtiness or hate etc.
3. It should not reflect un-Islamic ideas and inclinations.
4. It should not convey any improper and bad meaning like Aasia (The Sinner), Hariqa (The Burner) Harb (Tue war) etc.
5. It should not be degrading and disgraceful.
6. The names like Shahin Shah, Malik-ul-Mulk (Emperor) are the worst names.

The Holy Prophet said:

You would be called by your names and the names of your fathers. So give good names (to your children)".
(Abu Dawood).

The Names liked by Almighty Allah

According to Hazrat Abu Wahab the Holy Prophet said,

"Give (Your children) the names of the prophets of Allah. Almighty Allah likes most of the names of Abdullah and Abdur Rahman. Haris (cultivator or hand labourer) and Hammam (Determined) and steadfast are also good names. The most detestable names are Harb (War) and Murrah (Bitter Taste)". (Al-Adab Al-Mufrad).

Muslim Parents

Impression of Improper Names

Hazrat Yahya Ibne Saeed relates that once the Holy Prophet wanted someone to milk a she camel. He asked the people who were present at that time, "who will milk the camel"? A person stood up and offered his services. He asked his name which, was "Murrah". The Holy Prophet bade him to sit down. Another man came forward to do the job. He, too, was asked to tell his name, he told "Harb". The Holy Prophet asked him to take his seat and repeated the question for the third time. The third person who eagerly stood up to get the honour, his name was "Yaish" which means 'living long'. This was permitted to milk the camel.

(Imam Malik)

A similar Hadith is related by Imam Bukhari. According to him once Hazrat Mohammad (P.B.U.H.) asked some persons that who would carry his camel home. One of them offered his services. But after coming to know his name he did not select the man for the job. Another was also rejected due to his improper name. The third one who offered his services told the Holy Prophet that his name was Najiah (the delivered). The Holy Prohpet told the person, "You are the suitable person for this job. Carry the camel home."

Once Hazrat Umar asked the name of a person, he told "Fire". When asked his father's name, he replied "Flame". Hazrat Umar then asked the name of his tribe, the man said "The Burning". He then asked about his locality, he told "The hillock of Fire". Hazrat Umar further asked, "which hillock of Fire"? The man replied, "on the hillock of flaring fire". Hearing this Hazrat Umar said, "Rush home as all the persons of your

Giving Good Names To The Children

house have been burnt to death". When he reached home he found out that Hazrat Umar was exactly true. (Jama-ul-Fuwaid)

Respect for Names

Hazrat Abu Rafe quoted the Holy Prophet that he said,

"When you name someone Muhammad, neither beat him nor deprive him". (Jama-Al-Fawaid)

Similarly Hazrat Umar relates that the Messenger of Almighty Allah once admonished,

"You name your children Muhammad and then rebuke them too".

Some Names Suggested by the Holy Prophet Muhammad (S.A.W.)

1. Hazrat Yousuf, son of Abdullah-bin-Salam tells that his name was given by the Holy Prophet who took him in his lap and caressed his head with his hand.
(Al-Adab Al-Mufrad)

2. Hazrat Abu-Moosa relates that when his first son was born he took him to the Holy Prophet who gave him the name of Ibraheem. According to him the Holy Prophet prayed for him.
(Al-Adab Al-Mufrad)

The Holy Prophet gave considerable importance to the names. Whenever he came across improper and unmeaningful name he changed it to some proper one. He changed the names

Muslim Parents

of several men and women in this way. Hazrat Aisha relates that the Holy Prophet used to change improper names.

(Tirmizi)

Hani Ibn Zaid once came to the Holy Prophet with a delegation. During conversation he knew that his surname is Abul Hakam (Father of Arbitrator)". The Holy Prophet called him and said, "Why you adopted Abul-Hakam as your surname? It is Almighty Allah who is the only Hakam (The Judge Arbitrator). It is only he who judges. Ibne Zaid replied, "It is not so (that I want to share the right of Allah). In fact whenever the people of my tribe have any dispute or differences they come to me for decision. I decide the matter and the parties concerned readily accept my decision. The Holy Prophet said, "you have nicely interpreted". He then enquired, 'have you any child"? He said he had three sons named Shuraih, Abdullah and Muslim, of these three Shuraih was the eldest. The Holy Prophet said, Now your surname would be Abu Shuraih". He also prayed for him and his children. During the same meeting he came to know that one of the person from Zaids delegation was named Abdul-Hajar. He told the person that from now on, "Your name is Abdullah".

According to Shuraih when Hani Ibne Zaid was leaving for his home he came to the Holy Prophet and requested to tell him how could he be certain of entry into Heaven? He was told to take two steps for achieving that purpose. First he should speak politely and gently to others and secondly he should distribute as much food as possible (among the poor).

(Al-Adab Al-Mufrad)

Hazrat Abdul Rahman narrates that when he went to the

Giving Good Names To The Children

Holy Prophet for the first time, the Holy Prophet asked his name. He told his name as "Abdul Uzza". The Holy Prophet said, "No, your name is Abdul Rahman".

According to another version he told his name as "Azeez" to which the Holy Prophet replied, "Azeez is the title of Allah only". (Jama-Al-Fawaid)

According to Hazrat Ibne Umar the Holy Prophet changed the name of 'Aasia (sinner) to Jameela (Beautiful) (Al-Adab Al-Mufrad). She was the daughter of Hazrat Umar.

Once Hazrat Mohammad bin 'Amr went to the house of Zainab, the daughter of Abu Salmah. She asked the name of his sister who accompanied him. He replied that her name was Barrah. Zainab told him to change the name of his sister because after marrying Zainab-daughter of Jahash the Holy Prophet changed her name from Barrah (Pious) to Zainab. She further told him that when the Holy Prophet married my mother Umme Salmah, he heard her calling me by the name of Barrah. Hearing this he said, "Do not assert your piety. Only Allah knows better as who is pious and who is virtuous. Change her name to Zainab", to which her mother readily agreed. Hearing this the narrator asked Zainab to suggest any suitable name for his sister. She replied that she should be given the same name which was given by the Holy Prophet. And then he changed the name of his sister from Barrah to Zainab.

Hazrat Raitah, daughter of Hazrat Muslim quotes her father to have said that during the battle of Hunaim the Holy Prophet asked his name. He told him that his name was "Ghurab" (Crow). The Holy Prophet said, "No, your name is Muslim".

(Al-Adab Al-Mufrad)

Muslim Parents

Hazrat Aisha relates that once a person told the Holy Prophet that his name was Shihab (the Flame). The Holy Prophet changed his name to Hisham. (Al-Adab Al-Mufrad)

The name of the son of Abdul Rahman Bin Saeed Makhzoomi was "As-Saram" (the dropped crop) during his pre-Islamic life. When he embraced Islam the Holy Prophet changed his name to "Saeed" (Lucky). The Holy Prophet once asked Hazrat Saeed, "who is elder between us, I or you?" Hazrat Saeed replied, "you are elder to me and I am older (in age) than you." During his last days Hazrat Saeed lost his eyes. Once Hazrat Umar went to enquire about his health and asked him to come to the mosque for offering congregational and Juma prayers. He replied that his absence from the mosque is due to the non-availability of any companion who could accompany him to the mosque. Hearing this Hazrat Umar sent a slave for his guidance and service.

The Holy Prophet advised the people not to give the name "Habab" to their children for Habab is Satan. The infant is not a Satan but the slave of Allah. (Jama-ul-Fawaid). Habab means snake and that is why the world is called "Ummul Habab" - Mother of snakes. That is why the Holy Prophet has forbidden Muslims to give this name to their children.

Bad Effects of Bad Names

Hazrat Saeed Bin Musaiyib relates that once the Holy Prophet asked his grandfather his name. He replied that his name was "Hazn". He advised him to change his name to "Sahl". But Hazn declined to do so and said: it is the name given to him by his father so I am unable to change it. Hazrat Saeed says

Giving Good Names To The Children

that due to this reason the members of our family are still rough and headstrong.

'Hazn' means hard and uneven land and "Sahl" means 'soft and even land' above narrative proves that the name had its own effects upon the person who adopts it. Historians say that the members of the family of Hazn were extremely rude and harsh and remained so.

Calling One by a Good Name

We should always call a person by a good name. It often happens that in a moment of sheer love and affection we like to call a person by a name other than the actual one. At such time we should take care that such a name should be a pleasing one so that the person concerned should like it too. The Holy Prophet liked it most that every person should be called by the name or surname which he likes most. (Al-Adab Al-Mufrad)

Once the Holy Prophet went to the house of his son-in law Hazrat Ali and found that Hazrat Ali was out. He asked his daughter Hazrat Fatimah, wife of Hazrat Ali, where is the son of my uncle? She replied, "We had some altercation between us. He got angry with me and left the house. He did not have even siesta". The Holy Prophet asked someone to go and find out where Hazrat Ali was. The man came back and told that he was sleeping in the mosque. The Prophet of Allah went to the mosque and saw his son-in-law lying on his back upon the ground. He bent over him and wiping gently the dirt off his body and said, "Get up Abu Turab, Get up Abu Turab".

Calling by the Short Name

The Holy Prophet sometimes called his near and dear ones by their shortnames. For instance he would often call Hazrat

Muslim Parents

Aisha and Hazrat Usman as "Aish and 'Usm out of sheer love and affection. Hazrat Abu Salmah quotes Hazrat Aisha that once the Holy Prophet said to her, "O' Aish, this is Gibraeel (the Arch Angel) and offers salutation to you". She replied, "May Allah bless him too". She then said to Abu Salmah, "I was unable to see what the Holy Prophet was seeing (at that time)".

(Al-Adab Al-Mufrad)

Moreover there may be some situations when we want to call a person whose name is not known to us or we have forgotten it. We should call him/her by a good and pleasant word. Whenever the Holy Prophet would forget the name of a person whom he wanted to call he would call him by addressing "O' son of Abdullah (servant of Allah)."

Loving One's Children

One of the rights of children over their parents is that they should get full love and affection from them. Love for the children is an instinct which has been inculcated in the nature of all the parents by Almighty Allah. It shows and proves His kindness, wisdom and supremacy over the universe. Had it not been so how many of us would have survived at all? Nobody cares to take pains and bring up a helpless, new born infant except a man and a woman who are responsible for its birth—the parents. Not only the human beings but the animals too have been endowed with this natural love by the Creator. Actually the world—human and animal both—are surviving and owe their very existence to this basic and most important instinct.

Here it should be noted that all the parents have been gifted with this instinct without any consideration for their beliefs. But Muslim parents love and cherish their children considering it not only their natural duty but religious duty as a sunnat of the Holy Prophet and his holy companions. For them loving their children is not only the fulfilment of their natural desire but through this, they hope to earn the pleasure of Allah and His Holy Prophet and to get rewarded here and Hereafter. These elements make them love and cherish their children sincerely, selflessly and enthusiastically. This conscious love is very different from the love which is only instinctive. Muslim parents do not love their children blindly. They love their children according to the instructions given by Islam and never take such emotional steps which might prove disastrous for them or for their children.

Muslim Parents

Children - A Test for Parents

The love and affection for children is also a test for their parents. Almighty Allah, on the one hand, has created love in the hearts of parents and has also warned them to be careful of their children on the other. This warning is given due to the fact that these very children, sometimes, bring destruction to their parents. Such parents, for undue love for their children, lose all the differentiation between good and bad, right or wrong, due and undue, and vice and virtue. To provide more and more comforts and luxuries for their children they indulge in earning more and more money by all means which are unfair and prohibited by Islam. That is why Almighty Allah has cautioned us against loving our children to the extent that they might prove our enemies. According to the Holy Quran,

> "O' you who believe, verily of your wives and your children, (some are) enemy to you; wherefore beware of them". (64:14)

This warning tells us not to indulge in any sort of malpractices to provide more and more comforts and luxuries for our children. Our children become our enemies when our love for them leads us to immoral and irreligious activities. So we should always keep it in mind that we should restrain our love for children upto the limits imposed by Almighty Allah and His Holy Prophet. For these reasons the children are mentioned, in the Holy Quran as a Test or Trial for their parents. On the one hand there is the natural instinct of love for them and the demands of Islam on the other. We are commanded to fulfil our duties towards our children as well as to carry on the obligations required by our Faith. It is said in the Holy Quran,

Loving One's Children

"O' You who believe, let not your wealth, nor your children divert you from the remembrance of Allah; and whosoever do so, these are the losers".

(63:9)

This verse reminds us that the real loss of a person is that he destroys his life hereafter for the gains of this mortal world. So the Muslims should always keep this warning in mind and act accordingly.

Once the Holy Prophet was addressing a gathering in the mosque at Medina. Meanwhile his grandchildren Hazrat Hasan and Hussain came tottering towards him. He got down from the pulpit, brought the children to the pulpit and made them sit beside him. Then he said aloud, "Almighty Allah has truly said your wealth and your children are a test for you".

Hazrat Khola Bint Hakeem was a very pious woman. She relates that one day the Holy Prophet came out with one of his grandsons in his arms. He was saying to the child, "It is you who make people miser, it is you who make people coward and it is you who make people behave irrationally and unwisely".

(Tirmizi)

It is a fact that man falls prey to several weaknesses and waverings for the sake of his children. At times he acts like a coward and yields to certain pressures though he knows that he should not. Sometimes he hesitates to take a bold step merely for the sake of his children's future. He becomes a miser only for his children's sake and abstains from spending in the way of Allah. For earning and saving more and more for them he sometimes goes out of way and adopts unfair and illegal ways of earning. Islam does not ask its followers not to love their children or cater for their due needs and comforts. In fact it wants and makes the parents love their children as this attitude is liked and wanted by Almighty Allah and His Holy Prophet. But it does warn the parents to keep always in mind the instructions given by Almighty Allah and His Holy Prophet and not take any steps in the direction which is against the will of the creator. In other words Islam binds the parents to love their children as much as they can without exceeding the limits fixed by Almighty Allah.

> "Hazrat Anas narrates that once we, alongwith the Holy Prophet went to the house of Abu Saif (the blacksmith). He was the husband of the woman who was the foster mother of the Holy Prophet's son Hazrat Ibraheem. The Holy Prophet took his son in his arms, kissed him and put his nose on the face of the child. After sometime we saw that Hazrat Ibraheem was breathing his last and tears were rolling down from the eyes of the Holy Prophet. Seeing this Hazrat Abdur Rahman-bin-Auf said, "you too are weeping, O' Prophet of Allah"! He replied, "O Ibne Auf, these tears are sign of love and kindness". And the tears again started rolling down from his eyes. Then he said, "Though our hearts bleed and our eyes flow but we say (at such occasions) what our Allah likes. O Ibraheem we are very much grieved by your departure". (Bukhari, Muslim)

Cold Attitude Towards the Children

Some people do not laugh, play and treat merrily with their children. They think doing so is against piety and self respect. They have the false notion that if they kiss, embrace, play, laugh

Loving One's Children

or fondle with their children, they will lose their respect and fatherliness. To their mind the more they would avoid being pleasant and friendly with their children the more they will be respected. Rather they go to the extremes of being unconcerned, detached and even harsh with them. They think it below their dignity and status to be free and friendly with them. This attitude is neither required by Islam nor by the normal norms of social behaviour. Moreover this strict and harsh attitude of parents make them more repulsive and unpopular among their children. The whole parent - child relationship gets unbalanced, unhealthy and then creates a destructive distance between the two parties. Islam never approves this type of behaviour of the parents with their children. Rather this unwise, improper and harmful attitude clearly shows that such persons do not know Islam - their religion and their way of life. By their behaviour they prove that they are totally devoid of the comprehension and understanding of their religion. The Holy Prophet, by his behaviour and teachings, has clearly showed and taught the Muslims that loving our children by heart and deed is the most commendable practice. It also implies that persons, who do not make their children feel that they are really loved by them are totally lacking the virtues of love and kindness at all. Actually children are our most valuable assets and trusts. Parents who do not make their children believe, by their behaviour, that they love them sincerely are on the one hand creating socio-psychological troubles for themselves and their children and earning the displeasure of Almighty Allah on the other.

Loving the Children

Hazrat Abu Hurairah narrates, "The Holy Prophet once kissed his grandson Hazrat Hasan. Hazrat Aqra bin-Habis who,

Muslim Parents

was also present on the occasion, said that he had ten children but he had never kissed any one of them. The Holy Prophet looked at him and said, "Allah is never kind to him who is not kind to others". (Bukhari)

This Hadith denotes that kissing and fondling the children is the sign of love and kindness. Only kind ones do that. Almighty Allah is kind only to those who show their kindness to others. And those who are not kind to others do not deserve kindness from the Creator.

Hazrat Usama bin Zaid narrates that Hazrat Zainab sent a messenger to call her father, The Holy Prophet, with the message that her child was at the last breathes. The pious father told the messenger, "go back and give her my salutations and tell her that all which Allah gives and which he takes away belongs to Him. Everything takes place at the time fixed by Him. Have patience and be hopeful of getting rewarded by Him". Hazrat Zainab again called him under an oath which compelled him to go to her house. He was accompanied by Hazrat Sad-bin-Ubada, Muaz-bin-Jabal, Ubai-bin-Kab, Zaid-bin-Sabit and a few others. After reaching there the child was given to him. The child was breathing its last. Tears started rolling down from his eyes. Hazrat S'ad was surprised to see him weeping. The Holy Prophet said, "This is the love and kindness which Allah has put in the hearts of those who are kind to each other". Hazrat Aisha narrates that once a villager came to the Holy Prophet and asked, "Do you kiss your children? We never kiss our children." The Holy Prophet replied, "What can I do if Allah has extracted the feelings of kindness from your hearts".

(Bukhari, Muslim)

Hazrat Adi-bin-Sabit says he heard Hazrat Baraa saying,

Loving One's Children

"I saw Hazart Hasan sitting on the neck of the Holy Prophet and he was saying, O Allah I love him, may you too love him". Once one of his two grandsons Hazrat Hasan or Husain was sitting upon the shoulders of the Holy Prophet. Some one saw this and remarked, "what a nice riding"! Hearing the remarks the loving grandfather replied, "And what a nice rider too"!
(Seerat-Al-Nabi)

Hazrat Usama-bin-Zaid narrates that the Holy Prophet would take me and Hazrat Hasan in his arms and make us sit on and then his thighs hugging us would pray, "O' Allah be kind to both of them as I treat them with kindness". (Bukhari). He loved his grandsons Hazrat Hasan and Husain extremely and would often say that those were his "Bouquets". (Bukhari)

The Holy Prophet's Love for the Children

Hazrat Anas, the most sincere and faithful servant of the Holy Prophet, describes, "I never saw anyone who could love members of his family more than the Holy Prophet." (Bukhari)

Once the Holy Prophet was going somewhere when he saw Hazrat Hussain playing on the road. Hazrat Mohammad (P.B.U.H.) stopped and stretched out his both hands to take his grandson in his arms. Hazrat Hussain dodged and escaped his outstretched hands several times in order to tease his loving grandfather. At last he got hold of him. Then hugging him closely said, "Hussain belongs to me and I belong to Hussain".

Hazrat Zainab had a loving daughter named Umama. The Holy Prophet very much loved the child. She would often remain with him while he would offer prayers. During prayers she would sit on his shoulders. When bowed for Ruku, he would put her down and climb again on his shoulders when he stood.

Muslim Parents

Once somebody sent some gifts to the Holy Prophet which included a gold necklace. At that time Umama was also playing there. The Holy Prophet said that he would give the necklace to the one who was dearest to him in the family. Hearing this the members of the family thought that he would give the necklace to Hazrat Aisha. But, against all expectations, he called little Umama to him and put the necklace around her neck by his own hands.

An Incident about Hazrat Yaqoob

According to Hazrat Anas the Messenger of Allah told him that once someone asked Hazrat Yaqoob (P.B.U.H.) that how he lost his eyesight, and why his back was bent. Hazrat Yaqoob replied that he had lost his eyesight as he had been weeping incessantly for the absence of his son Hazrat Yousuf and his back bent due to the shock of detention of his other son Benyameen. Immediately Hazrat Gibraeel came to him and said, "Are you complaining against Almighty Allah"? He replied, "No, rather I am telling my woeful tale to Allah". Hazrat Gibraeel said that Almighty Allah already knew all what he was trying to tell Him, and then he went away. Hazart Yaqoob then entered his room and praying to Almighty Allah said, "O' my Lord! do you not pity on an old man? You have taken my eyesight and made my back bend with grief, O' Lord give me back my flowers (sons) so that I may smell them only once and then do whatever you like with me". Just then Hazrat Gibraeel again came to him and told him, "Almighty Allah sends Blessings upon you. He says, O' Yaqoob, be happy (with the greetings of giving you back your sons) had your sons even died We would have made them alive again for the sake of your joy and comfort".

(Targheeb-o-Tarheeb)

Education & Training of Children

No doubt, to provide the physical needs of children is a valuable and important duty for you. Inspite of being well fed and dressed, it is meaningless if they are not well trained and educated. You commit a gross negligence if you over-look this aspect. Your child's physical growth is a natural process while his mental and behavioural patterns are purely the social processes. He learns to speak, eat, dress, and behave as he is taught by the persons who nourish them. A child, at birth, is neither a saint nor a criminal. He becomes what he is made by the persons concerned. And these persons are no other than the parents. It depends upon them to make or destroy the life of their children. They are the first and foremost teachers of their little children. It is their most important duty to train and educate their children in most befitting manner so that they may become good Muslims, civilized, cultured, noble, gentle, law abiding and responsible citizens and important units of society in their future lives. They should educate their sons and daughters according to the Islamic teachings so that they may develop balanced and pleasant personalities and thus prove to be a source of pride and satisfaction for their parents.

The Role of Mother

Though father plays an important role in educating the child but mother plays a more important and greater role in this process. Rather it can rightly be said that the mother contributes the greater share and plays the best role in the early training and education of her children. Many a children, whose fathers were dead even before they were born, came out to be best persons and became an asset for the humanity due to the nurture and training of their mothers.

Usually the father mostly remains out on account of economic and other important pursuits. Particularly in this highly competitive and busy world of today man still spends most of his time outside home. Consequently he cannot devote himself to look after the children properly. Naturally, in these circumstances the mother finds ample opportunity to care for her children as she remains indoor nearly all the time. Moreover as the mother is more loving, kind and patient than the father, she is nearer to the children and they are more free and attached to her. They are open to her and thus all their likes and dislikes, capabilities and drawbacks are best known to her. This makes the mother most capable of educating and training her children in most proper way. Moreover the children usually react abnormally to the callous or strict treatment which a father metes them out. They become insolent, rebellious and wayward by the behaviour of their father who, due to the perplexities of life, becomes easily irritated with them. On the other hand the mother, who is given remarkable patience and forbearance by nature, brings them round with love, tolerance and affection. Thus the children respond to her more properly than to their father. They are more attached to their mother and confide in her their best secrets and problems which she can redirect into healthier channels and thus lightens the burdens from the hearts and minds of her children. Thus the mother can best help the children form healthier and proper habits and attitudes which are in tune with the time and circumstances.

Education & Training of Children

A Mother Transforms the Lives of People

Once a group of merchants was going to Baghdad. With them was also a young boy whose mother had given him some basic instructions for his safe future course of life. In their way they were attacked by a gang of dacoits who robbed them of their whole belongings. When the operation was over, one of the robbers spotted the young boy who was calm and quiet. He asked him if he had anything? The lad boldly replied that he had forty dinars with him. The robber was surprised by the bold and outright declaration of the boy. He could not believe that such a young lad had as much money about which he told him so plainly and quickly. He took the boy to his leader and told him the story. The leader too asked the boy about the money which he claimed to have with him. Again he replied in the affirmative without any hesitation. The man asked, "where the money is". The bold and truthful lad replied that the money lies in a purse stitched in his belt he wore. The purse was brought out from his belt which really contained forty dinars as told by the lad.

The leader surprisingly asked the boy where and why he was going? The lad replied that he was going to Baghdad for religious education and, as he was a complete stranger over there, his mother had given him this money to meet the expenses. Then the robber chief could not control his curiosity and enquired the lad that why did he not try to hide the money and told them so readily about it? The boy calmly replied that his mother had strictly advised him never to tell a lie and to be truthful in all circumstances. How could he disobey his mother, he added.

The reply stirred the conscience of the robber and made him think that the lad, knowing all the consequences unhesitatingly

Muslim Parents

spoke the truth under the instructions of his mother while he himself had been totally unheedful to the instructions of Almighty Allah through his repulsive deeds. He embraced the child, gave him and all the merchants their money back and fell down in prostration.....praying Almighty Allah for his forgiveness. The same robber became the most pious man and spent rest of his life in helping the poor and needy. The training of a great mother not only made her child great and famous but also made a robber change into a saint. And this child was later known to the world as Hazrat Abdul Qadir Jeelani, one of the greatest personalities of Islam.

Making The Future of Children

After having children, the first and foremost desire of parents is to prepare them for a bright and successful future. They leave no stone unturned to make their children live a happy and contended life. This is the natural desire of parents without an exception. This is also the most appropriate and commendable desire even from the religious point of view. Islam commands its followers to make the future of their children as good as possible. But here we should make it clear that how the preparation of a bright future is defined by Islam.

In order to find a precise answer to this question we will have to know the answer of another question - what is the difference between the desire of a Muslim and a non-Muslim to have children? This can successfully be understood by the verses in the Holy Quran pertaining to one of the Holy Messenger of Almighty Allah - Hazrat Zakaria. According to the Holy Quran:

> "He (Zakaria) said, "O' my Lord, verily my bones are weakened and my head does glisten with grey hairiness but never have I, in my prayer to you, O' my Lord, been unblessed. And verily I fear my kindred after me and my wife is barren. So grant me from yourself an heir who shall inherit me and inherit from the family of Yaqoob. And O' my Lord make him your favourite creature".
>
> (19:4-6)

Muslim Parents

Hazrat Zakaria and his wife, reaching at the last stages of their lives, felt gloomy of being childless. Particularly Hazrat Zakaria was much worried as there was none to bear the torch of his mission and propagate the Religion of Almighty Allah. He was observing that the younger generation had no one who could be true and proper successor as all of them were inattentive to his cause. So he prayed to the Creator to give him a son and not for any worldly or emotional reasons. That was why Almighty Allah accepted his prayer and gave him a son whose glorious future is witnessed by the Holy Quran:

> "And we gave him a wisdom while yet a child, and tenderness of heart from our self and purity. And he was pious and dutiful towards his parents. And he was not haughty and rebellious. (19:12-14)

According to the Holy Quran, Hazrat Yahya was endowed with the following virtues:

1. Power to decide correctly.
2. Tender heartness.
3. Purity.
4. God fearing life, obedience to parents.
5. Life free of transgression and disobedience.

We will discuss them one by one in detail and in the same order as described in the verse as these are the best virtues which definitely vouchsafe illuminating future for any person in the world.

1. Hukm means capability of taking correct decisions. Making just, judicious and appropriate decisions in religious and

Making The Future of Children

worldly affairs is a much valued and commendable capability.

2. Tender heartness and kindness is not only a virtuous trait itself but it also creates other moral qualities.

3. Purity means purity of soul and body. A man of pure character never digresses from the path of righteousness. His life was far away from sin, lewdness, transgression and shameful acts. This is also a rare and lofty quality.

4. Fear of Allah and piety leads to a successful life. It is the most wanted and lovely quality which has been repeatedly asked by Almighty Allah to be cultivated by us. Only one who fears Allah deserves to be honoured and blessed by Allah.

5. Obedience and respect for the parents enables a person to be dutiful and beneficent to the society. Only such a person who obeys and serves his parents, is conscious to his duties to parents, is loved by his parents. One who disobeys his parents can never earn the pleasure of Almighty Allah and parents.

Keeping all these virtues in view, we conclude that the glorious future of our children does not lie in providing them with the worldly comforts, lofty buildings, precious cars, educational certificates and degrees, high offices and material prosperity only. By these facilities they will no doubt become rich and comforted and the so-called educated persons and Islam does not forbid to achieve them, but if they lack in basic religious education and moral and ethical standards set by Islam, they can never be really successful and fully equipped with the qualities required for a balanced, normal and ideal life. We should never forget that the life of this world is neither the real nor the only one. For us, the Muslims, real life is not here but hereafter.. Actually this limited life on earth is our test by Our Creator. Everyone of us has limited span of life during which his every move, good or bad, is noted and recorded by the specially appointed angels of Almighty Allah. Our real life will start from the day of Resurrection when we all will be reconstructed from our graves and brought before Almighty Allah for Judgement. This will be the real future of us and our children for which they should be prepared. It means that they should be given proper religious as well as other education so that they may be able to lead their lives as a true Muslim and may succeed well in both the lives, here and hereafter.

Islam and Character Building of Children

To make our children's life successful according to the standards set by Islam, we should vigorously and devotedly train and educate them. We should carry on our duty with wisdom, affection, patience and steadfastness. Our labour would exalt our position in the eyes of Allah and our status in the society. The Holy Prophet said:

> "The best gift which a father gives to his children is that of their good education and manners."

Parents will continuously and increasingly be rewarded in Afterlife by Almighty Allah for these efforts. The Holy Prophet says;

Making The Future of Children

"When a person dies his behaviour also comes to an end. But there are three things done by him for which he goes on getting the reward from Allah. First one is he who leaves some charitable trust for the benefit of the people, secondly he leaves behind some knowledge which is continuously useful for the people and thirdly, he leaves behind a pious son who goes on praying for his forgiveness".

On another occasion he said:

"The parents of a person who acquired extensive knowledge of the Holy Quran and practised accordingly will be crowned on the last day and this crown will shine more than the bright sun which lightens all the houses of the world. So what do you think about the person who behaves like this"?

(Abu Dawood, Hakim)

According to another Hadith narrated by Hazrat Buraidah the Holy Prophet said:

"The parents of the person who studied, learned and practised the Holy Quran will wear shining crown which will shine like the sun. And his parents will wear such precious dresses which will cost more than the total riches of the whole world. Then they will be surprised by this honour and they will enquire that for what they are honoured. They will be told that, this is the reward for the knowledge of Holy Quran which their child acquired."

Thus the Messenger of Allah has induced the parents to make their children learn and practise the Holy Book for which they will be lavishly rewarded by Almighty Allah. The purpose underlying the suggestions is that no child should lack the religious education and every child should adopt the habit of passing his whole life according to the education and knowledge thus acquired. It also implies that parents who neglect the education and training of their children will be questioned and punished for their negligence.

Consideration for the Self-Respect of the Children

Hazrat Abdullah-bin-Abbas narrates that the Holy Prophet said, "Be kind to your children and give them proper education". (Ibn-e-Majah)

Here the Holy Prophet directs the parents not only to educate and train the children but be kind to them. To be kind to one's children is as important that it has been given precedence to education. 'To be kind' means that the parents should so behave their children that their ego and self-respect may not be injured and they do not consider themselves as useless. Callous, overstrict and bitter attitude of parents make their children an easy prey to the feelings of inferiority. Once afflicted with this dangerous and destructive complex their whole lives are ruined. They start developing various psychological disturbances which establish them as misfits in the society. Feelings of self-respect start developing in the child just after his birth. If he is beaten, rebuked and neglected he would certainly go down in his own eyes and loose his self-respect for the rest of his life. He will not be able to have confidence in himself and thus becomes weak, nervous and even neurotic. Such children, even after coming of age, become a burden on society and instead of

Making The Future of Children

making any commendable contribution they pose serious threat to the welfare of the society.

The unkind the callous attitude of the parents often makes their children rebellious, wayward and even aggressive. These children start hating their parents and whenever they get an opportunity to make them uneasy and restless they avail it fully and without fail. These very children, after some years, come out to be adolescents but only to be labelled as delinquents. And these adolescents, with the passage of time, become hardened criminals. Some of them go to the mental hospitals and still several of them are seen on the streets being teased and pelted with stones by the children around them.

Thus we have to keep in mind these dire consequences of being unfair and unkind to our children who, if treated unfairly and unkindly, either become the upholders of vice and crime or become total nervous wrecks and neurotics. That is why it is a universal truth that parents are the makers as well as destroyers of the personalities of their children. Their minds, upto the first few years, are like the fresh and clean unexposed films. Whatever the parents say or do with them, gets permanently transferred to and imprinted on these films never to be dimmed in future. Their whole personalities are developed under these very impressions. Consequently it is our duty to assess our behaviour with our children and make ourselves habitual of being kind, fair and reasonable with them so that they could possess balanced and pleasant personalities.

The Holy Prophet, while emphasising the need of religious and general education of children, has also warned the parents and guardians that would definitely be questioned by Almighty

Allah to this effect. Islam demands all the parents as well as the guardians to arrange for the proper education and socialization of their children and dependents. He has said:

> "One who is made the guardian of less or more individuals, will definitely be questioned by Almighty Allah, on the Day of Judgement, that whether he made his subordinates to follow the path of Islam or ruined them. He would be questioned even about his family members."

Time for Education of Children

Education starts right from the birth of a child. Rather the first few years are extremely important and rightly called the formative years of life. Unfortunately we usually waste these decisive years of the lives of our children either due to carelessness or some other socio economic reasons. The underlying motive of performing the sunnat of calling Azan into the ears of a child just after birth is to imprint the notion of greatness and supremacy of Almighty Allah upon the mind of the infant right from the beginning of life on this earth. Allama Ibn Qaiyim, in his book, "Tuhfatul Wadood" writes about this Sunnat:

> "Its purpose is that the first words which an infant hears should convey the Greatness and Supremacy of Almighty Allah which would be the foundation of his conscious faith later on, as at the end of his life we exhort him to recite Kalimah-i-Tauheed. Secondly, by this important act, the Satan who wants to insinuate a Muslim right from his birth takes to his heels immediately hearing Azan and Iqamat and thus the infant gets the Message of Islam and Allah's worship before the misleading call of the Satan."

Making The Future of Children

Though an infant cannot speak but he definitely learns by whatever he hears and sees around him. He learns a lot from his mother through his sensory perceptions. Hence even during infancy, nothing should be said or done which we do not want to be learnt by the child. During this period he should hear nice words and recitations from the Holy Quran. As soon as the child learns to speak he should be taught Kalimah-i-Tauheed with its translation in his mother tongue so that from the very beginning he should have a clear idea and belief in the oneness of Almighty Allah. It is related that the Holy Prophet made it a tradition to teach, every child of his family who learned to speak, the following verse from the Holy Quran:

> "He, who has the kingdom of heavens and the earth and He has not taken (to Himself) any son, and there is none who shares with Him the kingdom, and He created everything and then He planned (for everything) a fixed measure". (25:2)

This brief verse is one of the most compact and comprehensive verses from the Holy Quran. If a child is taught this verse with its meaning in the beginning, he will definitely prove himself true Muslim throughout his whole life.

> According to another Hadith the Holy Prophet said:
> "When your children should start speaking make them learn Kalima-i-Tauheed,
> LA ILLAHA ILL-LAL-LAH MUHAMMAD-UR-RASOOL-UL-LAH
> (There is no god save Allah, Muhammad (P.B.U.H.) is His Messenger)

Religious Education of Children

When the children start speaking well they should be taught about Salat prayers and supplications. They should be made to learn all the verses and essentials of Salat with translation so that they could also understand the meaning of what they say. Great care should be taken that they pronounce the words correctly because words mispronounced in this age cannot easily be corrected later on. The Holy Quran should also be taught to them at the same stage. Make them memorise some verses as well as the translation and meaning of these verses from the Holy Quran. This would make them realise the importance of the Holy Quran and they will acquire the habit of reading and understanding it with care, interest and accuracy.

Moreover we should also teach them the Prophet's supplications meant for different occasions like going to bed, eating and drinking, wearing new clothes, sneezing by one's ownself and by others, going to the natural calls and coming back, beginning and ending the fast and seeing the new moon etc. These things go a long way in moulding the children into Islamic way of life.

Furthermore, at this stage, the parents should also teach their children manners and etiquettes demanded by religion and society. The children have to be socialized in order to cope with the various situations which they will face living in the society. This moral and social training will make them adjust themselves with different situations and circumstances. They should be prepared to come up to the general standards and expectations of the society so that they could live their lives with normally and success. They should be made deft in the art of living which

Making The Future of Children

is most important for living a successful life in society. They should be taught the ways and manners of cleanliness, sleeping, talking, walking, reading, writing, playing and various other matters which they will face during their later lives. Too much of moral and ethical lecturing often bores the children and gradually loses its importance. The best way of making your children learn things you want them to learn is to practice them yourself. Then they will easily and automatically emulate what they will see being done by you. Parents are the best ideals for their children. They readily adopt the manners and movements, ways and procedures adopted and acted upon by their parents. So it goes without saying that the parents should themselves bear all the qualities which they want to see in their children.

Hazrat Umar-bin-Abu Salma was the son of the wife of Hazrat Mohammad (P.B.U.H.) Hazrat Umm-i-Salma. He was brought up by the Holy Prophet. He related,

> 'Once, during my childhood, I was sitting in the lap of the Holy Prophet eating something. I was eating from all sides of the plate. The Holy Prophet advised me to say Bismillah (start by the Name of Allah) and then eat with the right hand and from just before me. Since then I have made it my habit.'

Telling True and Character Building Stories to the Children

Children are usually interested in listening stories during the period of their childhood. Sometimes they are so much interested in them that they want to adopt these characters which they like most in these stories. So the parents should take care in the selection of such stories and anecdotes for their children. They should always select meaningful, constructive and healthy stories so that they could teach desired lesson to their children through them. Particularly they should be told various events in an interesting way, from the lives of the Holy Prophet, religious personalities and national heroes to motivate them towards emulating the virtues contained in those true stories. It is a very effective way of teaching. Unfortunately, even now, some of the parents and others mislead and misguide the children by telling them the traditional stories about magic, Gennies, Demons, fairies, witches and other imaginary and mythological characters. These stereotype stories are extremely damaging to the innocent and tender minds of children. They make them cowards and afraid of non existing things. This is a slow poison which injects the mind of children and make them superstitious throughout their whole lives. Such unfounded fears get hold of their minds and no later education or reasoning can alleviate these fears from their brains. They lose the spirit of adventure and courage. Belief in one God-Allah teaches us to fear none save Allah, but these imaginary stories make the innocent children victim of unfounded fears. Sooner we do away with such stories, better it is.

The Salat (Prescribed Prayers)

Offering salat is the most important worship which keeps a Muslim closely attached with the Creator. It guards the religion, attracts to the observance of religious duties and prepares for the adoption of religion as way of life. Therefore right from the age of seven year the children should be made habitual of offering salat regularly. Leniency should never be adopted in this respect. Children should not be allowed to go to bed without

Making The Future of Children

offering Isha (night) prayers. If they go to sleep without offering this prayer they should be awakened and made to perform it. Parents should wake them up early in the morning for offering the Fajr (Morning) prayers so that they may become habitual of it. Almighty Allah says:

> "And enjoin the prayer on members of your family and be constant therein. (20:132)

The Holy Prophet also asks his followers thus;

> "Enjoin upon your children to offer Salat when they become seven years old and punish them when they reach to the age of ten (if they show slackness in offering salat) and also make them sleep separately at this age."

These instructions clearly mean that you too should be **regular** in offering salat and also make the environment of your **home conducive** to the offering of salat by your children. Moreover **you should** make it clear to them that you will never allow **the least slackness** on their part in this regard.

The Marriage of Children

As soon as the children cross the childhood and get the adolescence, the parents' responsibilities and anxieties take a new turn. When their sons are fully grown up, the parents feel elated by the thought that now these sons will help them and share their responsibilities. They start dreaming a home full of happiness and joy as their sons after getting married will bring pious, beautiful and obedient daughters-in-law for them. In case of daughters they, on the one hand, become worried to marry them off and get good husband for them while their hearts start sinking by the thought their beloved daughters would be separated from them and belong to another house for ever. The marriage of children is the social responsibility as well as the natural desire of the parents.

Islam also asks the parents to fulfil this responsibility when their children come to that age. It advises you to arrange for the marriages of your eligible children without any unnecessary delay. Though it definitely takes some time to find out a suitable match, but it asks you not to lose any more time once you have found a suitable match for your children specially when there is no major hitch to do so. The point stressed here is that unnecessary delay and negligence in this important matter, sometimes creates ugly situations for the parents, ultimately the responsibility lies on the parents.

Consequences of Unnecessary Delay in Marriage

As soon as a son or daughter gets adulthood, it is the fore-

The Marriage of Children

most duty to find out a suitable match for them and marry them at the earliest. Unnecessary and uncalled for delay in this important matter often causes shameful situation for the parents too. Particularly if a female digresses even once from the path of virtue she loses her dignity for ever. She carries the stigma of shame and disrespect along with her parents. In such cases the parents are not only looked down by the society, they are also held sinners in the eyes of Islam. According to an Hadith,

> "One who is bestowed with children by Almighty Allah, he should give them good names, give them good education and training and get them married when they gain adulthood. In case they are not married and digress from the path of virtue the father will be held responsible for that". (Baihaqi)

According to another **Hadith, the** Holy Prophet said:

> "It has been **ordained** in Torah that a **father, whose** daughter reaches **the age** of twelve and due to the **delay** in marriage indulges in wrong behaviour, will bear the responsibility for the sin committed by his daughter".

Finding a Suitable Match

Delay in the marriage of children usually happens due to the non-availability of a suitable match. No doubt it is the duty of parents to select most appropriate matches for their children. Islam also wants them to do so. It does not ask you to be so hurried in this connection as not to care for the suitability of the matches for their children. Marriage is one of the most important issues and it should be done very carefully and judiciously. Success or destruction of one's whole life temporal as well as Hereafter, depends upon the appropriate selection of the life partners to be bound in the sacred bonds of matrimony.

The thing to be taken care of in this regard is that the standards of our selection should be in accordance with Islam. It is quite possible that the marriage of your children is being delayed due to some unreasonable standards, fixed by you for the selection of a girl or a boy, which have no significance at all in Islam.

Basic Standards for Selecting Spouses

Usually there are five basic things which are taken into consideration while selecting a spouse. These are:

1. Financial Position.
2. Race and lineage
3. Beauty.
4. Religious and Moral Background.
5. Education.

No doubt each one of these things is important and matters most in matrimonial purposes. Nobody can deny the importance of the financial position of particularly the boy with whom a girl is to be married. Race and good families also cannot be overlooked as they make a lot of difference in the matters of thinking, customs and traditions which make marriage a success or a failure. The consideration for a beautiful and good looking, particularly a fair coloured girl is a general feature. And it is but natural that everybody likes beauty as it appeals to the aesthetic sense of all human beings. Education, specially in the modern times, is given much importance and has become a

The Marriage of Children

valuable feature in these matters. And it is needless to say that education brings a lot of changes in the behaviour of men and women and enables them to have more balanced, happy and contended lives. Through education they come to know and master the art of living which is absolutely necessary for each and every individual for living a successful social life. Superiority of man over all other creatures depends upon education and education alone. Religious and moral background is a must for all of us. Being Muslims we can never even imagine to marry our sons and daughters to those who are devoid of Islamic values and the moral and ethical standards taught by this impeccable and best religion.

Consequently if you get such a match for your sons and daughters who bears all these qualities, be thankful to Almighty Allah for being the most lucky person in the world. No gift in the whole world is better than this one. But practically speaking it is most unlikely, rather impossible to have all these qualities in an individual. Now it is upto you that which of these qualities you prefer most in selecting a spouse for your child. But one thing which is always kept in mind is that you must make such selections according to the requirements and standards established by Islam and prefer the same qualities which are preferred by our religion.

Advice of the Holy Prophet

Regarding this important issue the Holy Prophet has advised to give first preference to the quality of religious and moral perfection in the selectees. After this if any of the remaining four qualities are found the selectors are extremely lucky and they should thank the Creator for being so fortunate. We should not then delay in finalizing the marriage. In case the above mentioned quality is lacking in the person being selected for the purpose, he or she should no doubt be rejected even if all the other qualities are found in that person. If one lacks the basic and important quality of religious and moral disposition, he can never be considered a normal and responsible member of society. How can we even imagine to select such person to be the husband or wife of our daughter and son respectively. Many marriages have proved complete failures between the persons who lacked this vital quality. On the other hand there are thousands of couples in our society who are living a happy, balanced and contended marital lives in spite of lacking in beauty, affluence and modern higher education. And they owe this remarkable and enviable success to their religious consciousness and moral disposition which they abundantly possess. All the other related defects and deficiencies can be compensated and balanced by this one single virtue. But all the other capabilities and qualities can never compensate the dearth of religion and morality. The last Messenger of Allah has advised us thus:

> "For marriage usually four things are to be found in a girl - firm financial position, respectable family, beauty and Islamic morality. Marry a religious woman, may you live in peace".

This Hadith tells you to find such a bride for your son who is religious and equipped with Islamic standards of morality. Only such wives can make their homes full of Islamic environment and give birth to children who will uphold and uplift the glory of Islam.

The Marriage of Children

In the same way the Holy Prophet has also advised his followers to give importance to the same quality while selecting the bridegrooms for their daughters. Hazrat Abu Hurairah narrates, the Holy Prophet said:

> "Accept the proposal and marry your beloved daughter to the person whose religious and moral behaviour satisfies you. If you will not do so the society will suffer the worst disturbance."

This saying of the Holy Prophet Muhammad (P.B.U.H..) clearly denotes that if the boy, who wants to marry your daughters, is pious and gentle, religious minded and has Islamic standards of morality should readily be given the hand of your daughter in marriage without further quest for other qualities in him. For in the matter of marriage the quality which should be given overriding preference is the Islamic way of thinking and behaviour. All other considerations come later. The society, in which only wealth and beauty will be given importance in matrimonial matters and these or other things will be given preference over Islamic spirit and culture, will not take a long time to be disturbed and disintegrated.